D1536273

From
TORTURE to
TRIUMPH

The Lost Legend of a Man Who Opened America: Guillaume Couture

MICHAEL FENN

Copyright © 2015 Michael Fenn.

All rights reserved. No part of this book may be reproduced, stored, or transmitted by any means—whether auditory, graphic, mechanical, or electronic—without written permission of both publisher and author, except in the case of brief excerpts used in critical articles and reviews. Unauthorized reproduction of any part of this work is illegal and is punishable by law.

ISBN: 978-1-4834-3264-9 (sc)
ISBN: 978-1-4834-3263-2 (e)

Because of the dynamic nature of the Internet, any web addresses or links contained in this book may have changed since publication and may no longer be valid. The views expressed in this work are solely those of the author and do not necessarily reflect the views of the publisher, and the publisher hereby disclaims any responsibility for them.

Cover photo: Brendan Fenn

Lulu Publishing Services rev. date: 07/06/2015

Dedication...

For Fiona Mattea and Anne Madeleine, and all those
thousands of young Couture descendents around North
America who may be inspired by the courage and vision
of their intrepid ancestor, the "worthy Couture".

CONTENTS

PROLOGUE

Explorers, settlers and pioneers:

Our literature and popular entertainment are filled with legends and stories of those intrepid Europeans who first explored the New World. They braved the unknown, encountered unfamiliar peoples and cultures, and endured the hardships of the wilderness. In their own time, reports of their discoveries enlivened and enlightened a curious European audience – an intrigued readership of adventurers and evangelists, dispossessed farmers and penurious townsfolk, traders and speculators. But those explorers often left little to show for their adventures, beyond stirring tales, tantalizing artifacts, abandoned outposts, battles won and then lost, and many, many unmarked graves.

Real roots in North America were sunk with permanent settlement – by people who arrived as Europeans, but stayed to become 'Americans' – and Canadians.

When early settlers did come to stay, rather than just explore, they established themselves in isolated outposts, like rookeries on the jagged edges of a hostile North America. These little colonies carved-out a few thousand acres from old-growth forest or on rocky headlands and harbours, and then tried to survive surrounded by a vast and seemingly trackless wilderness. Their relations with the numerous Native peoples were fraught with a volatile mélange of suspicion, confusion, arrogance, apprehension and animosity.

In the early years, during the 17th century, newly arrived Europeans left most of the vast wilderness to the Natives. Whether Captain John Smith in Virginia, the Pilgrims at Plymouth and Salem, the Dutch at New Amsterdam or the French at Québec, European settlements remained hemmed-in by natural barriers and by the unpredictable belligerence of others in this New World, both Aboriginal and European. Until a way could be found safely to expand their farming and commerce into the rich hinterland, settlers and traders were few in numbers and their settlements were closely circumscribed.

There were exceptions. An extraordinary few formed the necessary bridge between mere exploration and extensive colonization. Without these essential, "linking" historical figures, the European explorers of North America would likely have been as ephemeral in their local impact as Livingston on Africa, Marco Polo on China, or De Soto in Arkansas and LaSalle in Texas.

The path out from that string of coastal palisades and forest forts was carved by a third and most vital category of the early Europeans in North America, who linked the explorer with the settler – the pioneer.

Pioneers in America

Pioneers may have been few in number, but they were the essential breakthrough between exploration and colonial settlement. In the Americas, their names festoon the familiar history of the 18th and 19th centuries. But their role was even more crucial in the 16th and 17th centuries. Whether their native tongue was English, Dutch, Spanish, Portuguese – or French, they were the newcomers who turned Europeans into americanos, canadiens and Yankees – "Americans" all.

Early pioneers combined the adventurous and practical way-finding of the explorer, with a capacity to blaze a trail that settlers could follow. Often among the first settlers themselves, the pioneers' courage and perseverance cleared the way for the more numerous and more prudent settlers who would follow. More darkly, they were often also the unknowing purveyors of European contagions that would decimate the Native population and fatally weaken the ability of Aboriginal nations to resist the encroachment of settlers. With first-encounters and simple trading, pioneers also introduced global economic and cultural forces that would fundamentally alter and ultimately nearly destroy a traditional Aboriginal way of life. *[See endnote respecting Aboriginal terminology.]*

These early European pioneers explored and embraced America in a new way. They often learned the languages and understood the cultures of those they encountered. Navigating this new world with courage, confidence and familiarity, they used its assets and learned its secrets to survive the perils of unknown wilderness lands and their peoples. They saw America not as a foreboding and inhospitable ocean of wilderness, but as an inviting river to be navigated and explored.

The most successful early pioneers enjoyed a unique capacity to live with and as part of the New World, rather than trying to conquer it or fundamentally change it. For them, the New World was just that: a new world. It was an unlimited, fresh, new place where the gifts of nature and openness to discovery let pioneers breathe the air of freedom. As with the generations that followed, America offered the intrepid opportunities unavailable in Europe's class-ridden, religiously intolerant, decaying and fetid cities and villages, and on the feudal farms that surrounded them.

It took raw courage and resilient spirit, combined with sensitivity to the unfamiliar and an inquiring mind – a marvelous combination no more common in their day than ours. But without that kind of pioneer, the "European" history of North America might well have read more like the colonial history of Central Africa, China or India.

We know them from our schoolbooks and popular myth. From the late 17th century through the early 19th century, they were the truly pioneering people of the New World. Embracing the wilderness and the wide spaces, establishing permanent and expanding communities for agriculture, fishery and forestry – philosophically looking forward into the interior – "to the west" – rather than over their shoulders, back across the ocean.

Their names – and those of their religious and royal patrons – populate our modern maps and give names to the communities that they built: the twelve LeMoyne brothers of Montréal – including Pierre d'Iberville (d. 1702) and his more long-lived younger brother Jean-Baptiste de Bienville (d. 1767) – founders of Mobile and New Orleans; Duluth, and La Vérendrye and his four sons, who in the 1700s built forts and established trade routes from Lake Superior to Wyoming; the agents of the Hudson's Bay Company and the North West Company – David Thompson, Simon Fraser, Samuel Hearne, and Alexander Mackenzie – who for two centuries after 1670 established a European presence from northwestern Québec and

Ontario, to the Pacific coast and into the Arctic; Daniel Boone (d. 1820) and Davy Crocket (d. 1836) crossing the Appalachians and opening the American heartland to American-born, English-speaking settlers; John Graves Simcoe (d. 1806) overseeing the settlement of frontier Ontario with Tory refugees from the War of American Independence; and, the Mormons in Utah (1847) and other settlers of the Far West territories, many newly seized from Mexico, or in the northwest, surrendered by Britain and Russia.

These people, however, 'stood on the shoulders' of earlier, more crucial, but often less remembered pioneers. Others had already settled Virginia, New Netherlands and New England; New France, Acadia, Haiti and the Antilles; the Spanish Main and Mexico. The pioneers from the 17th century made modern North America possible.

The "French Connection"

For both the scholar and the merely curious, there is an enigma about the omnipresent role of the French in the settlement of America, even in the US South, the mid-West and the Far West. History recounts that Spanish-speaking and English-speaking settlement was fought and won in the face of a determined and largely futile Native resistance, in a sad saga replete with betrayal, slavery, pandemics, 'ethnic cleansing', and in some cases, extermination.

So why were the French – far less numerous and with fewer resources – able to move across the continent and among the Native people for two centuries, almost like fish in the sea?

In the 18th and 19th centuries, we see the French – often anonymously – absorbed into many of the early American and British exploration and trading parties. Certainly, without the French Canadians in the Corps of Discovery, and notably Toussaint Charbonneau and his wife, Sacagawea, it is unlikely that Louis and Clark would have seen the Pacific, and the history of Northwest America might have been quite different. With their 'canadienne' or Native wives, and their sons and daughters, the French populated significant communities in the Canadian West and into the Northern States.

French place names still festoon our maps, from Des Moines IA, Eau Claire WI, Des Plaines IL, Duluth MN, and Detroit MI, as well as the French rendering of Native names "Chicago" and "Illinois", and moving south to St. Louis and St. Joseph in Missouri, Baton Rouge and New Orleans in Louisiana, Bay St. Louis and Biloxi in Mississippi, and Mobile in Alabama. French names find themselves assigned to Native peoples, as far flung as the Nez-Perce in Idaho, the Sioux on the Great Plains, and the Wyandotte in the mid-West.

A clue to this legacy lies in the unique approach adopted by the French. French pioneers consistently studied and adapted to Native culture and customs. Where they introduced European practices, like trade and religion, they frequently and successfully modified them to reflect an understanding of Native culture and values. Initially, the French came by their distinctive *modus operandi* almost by accident, aided by the foresight of Champlain, the Founder of Québec. The French approach was, in part, an inevitable consequence of their relatively small numbers (in relation to the English or the Spanish), the challenging climate of their location in northern North America, and the geographic ambitiousness of both their religious objectives and their primary commercial enterprise, the fur trade.

How that accident of history occurred has its roots in the pioneering work of Samuel de Champlain. From the beginning of New France in 1608, Champlain persuaded Native leaders to allow newly arrived French adolescents, like Étienne Brûlé (d. 1633) to live among them – sharing their hardships, learning their languages, absorbing their folklore and survival techniques. In the process, the Native people came to understand more about the French than the other Europeans, and often to adopt their prejudices about the others.

For the French, initially alien customs became more accessible. Elements of Native life came to make a great deal of sense in the perilous natural environment in which they found themselves. In fact, a number of Frenchmen, such as Brûlé (beginning in 1608) gave themselves over to the Native way of life, and abandoned their connection to the colony. Later, the "couriers-du-bois" – the so-called "forest runners" – ignored French colonial injunctions against unlicensed fur trading, moving into the wilderness and adopting the Aboriginal lifestyle. Ironically, in doing embracing the Native world so completely, they added to the spread of

French influence, knowledge and trade across a vast, unchartered continent in a way that would have been unthinkable using the formula devised in Paris by the "Old Regime".

But that was for the future. Given that by the time of his death in 1635, Champlain's Québec was reduced to a few hundred souls besieged behind palisades, the real explanation for this great historical transformation is better sought in the lives of a few remarkable people who immediately followed him.

This is the saga of one of the most remarkable of those people: one of the greatest and yet least known of America's (and Canada's) early pioneers. He was a man whose legacy arguably contributed to the basis for a new world in the New World.

CHAPTER 1

America: a thousand leagues away

The view from Rouen

Vivid blue highlights illuminate spectacular medieval stained-glass windows in the ancient church of St-Godard. Those windows have survived time and air raids – piercing the dark gothic interior and revealing the delicately painted wooden ceiling of the anonymous carpenters of Rouen. The windows are a hidden treasure of a church that still casts its shadow over the busy neighbourhood of St-Godard, in the ancient capital of Normandy – Rouen. In the cold January of his sixteenth birthday in 1633, Guillaume Couture looked up from his carpenter's apprentice bench in the shadow of St-Godard's spires, wondering about the world beyond those towering church walls.

History has been Normandy's glory and its burden. In the 17th century, Rouen was a crossroads of centuries-old contests – between the English and the French, between Huguenot Protestants and royalist Catholics, between merchants and landed nobles. Symbolic of its turbulent and intermingled history, Rouen's celebrated Gothic cathedral – a few city blocks from Guillaume Couture's father's carpenter shop – enshrined King Richard the Lionheart's legendary heart, while in Guillaume's own neighbourhood, a 13th century tower commemorated the burning, in Rouen's Old Market, of a 'heretic' known as Joan of Arc. Like many boys of his era, Guillaume (William) was named after Guillaume Le Conquérant, or in English, William the Conqueror, the most famous of Norman Dukes, who seized the English throne in 1066.

Guillaume Couture was born into a France that had recently concluded a century of the aptly named Wars of Religion – recurrent communal and local warfare of the most unforgiving, town-against-neighbouring-town variety. Inhumane excesses of violence – of the sort too often justified by claiming to act on God's behalf, even in our own day – cast a long shadow. There were fresh reminders of the intense underlying regional rivalries of class, commerce and politics that were the special curse of Normandy and Brittany. As Guillaume would later learn first-hand, however, indulging in religiously and culturally sanctioned torture, revenge and murder was not peculiar to Europeans.

Although France seemed mired in the past, new breezes were blowing nearby. Along the Channel and beyond the Pyrenees, Portugal, Spain, England and the Netherlands were exploring new lands, particularly in the exotic Americas, while France had been focused inward, preoccupied with enervating, internecine strife.

All Norman and Breton boys and girls had heard exciting tales of the High Seas and the Spanish Main from their relatives and local seamen. Stories were told of enduring great storms in small boats – of sea-monsters, pirates, cities of gold in Peru and Mexico – and of strange, exotic peoples mistakenly called both savages and Indians. With books increasingly available in the early 17th century, imaginations were fueled by the remarkable first-encounter drawings of the vanished Saturiwa Indians of south Florida, immortalized in Jacques Le Moyne de Morgues' detailed sketches of ferocious, tattooed Natives and exotic villages and customs – one of the first popular anthropological books since the invention of the printing press.

A keen observer and adept self-instructor, young Guillaume was one of the few in his father's carpentry guild who had learned to read. Reading opened wider worlds to the young apprentice. One of the local students, perhaps René Goupil from Anjou, had likely made available to him Samuel de Champlain's latest evocative and detailed 1632 book *"Voyages from western New France, called Canada"*, now in general circulation in Normandy.

Champlain, the Founder of Québec, would inspire and lift the horizons of Guillaume and many others in western France in the 1630s and 1640s, despite his own death in Québec on Christmas Day, 1635.

Woven among the adventure stories of Champlain, reading seems to have introduced Guillaume to conceptual thinking. In our era, when the promising child of a lower middle-class family can go to university, we might take this as unremarkable. For his time, Guillaume's capacity to reflect on the broader context and strategic implications of the situations that he observed was truly rare, even among the more educated nobility. His insights and his subtle, experience-based understandings ultimately proved to be so valued that they overcame the virulent prejudices of culture, history, religion and class. Throughout his life, Guillaume's counsel lifted him from the pre-ordained station to which the world typically and instinctively assigned him and others like him.

A New World beyond the Seas

As with so many in the 17th century and thereafter, America held great allure for a young person in Europe and Britain. It appealed to every adolescent's desire for adventure and excitement. At home, if they were poor, they faced a life of monotonous drudgery; even among the bourgeoisie and the minor nobility, the future presaged a life of stultifying predictability. For a tradesman with no social connections, the New World might allow your talents and your ambition to determine your life, rather than seeing it predetermined by your lack of a titled name, your regional accent, your guild affiliation, or your family's poverty.

Tales of adventure on the high seas and in the Americas were the currency of the docks and town squares of Normandy. Young Guillaume knew that Champlain and his partners had been trying to colonize French outposts in America for nearly thirty years. For most, the subsequent stories of death and privation had been enough to persuade even very destitute French peasants and townspeople to resist the siren call of Champlain's invitation. They would take their chances with a hard life in France.

Between the founding of the town of Québec in 1608 and the early 1630s, the population of New France had ebbed and flowed, comprised more of seasonal traders and fishermen than permanent settlers. When Guillaume read Champlain's book around 1633, the colony had just been restored to France by England. The population of the town of Québec had dropped to a mere seventy-seven Europeans, with only one permanent family in place, the Hébert-Couillard farming clan. (The Héberts had gone out to Québec in the year of Couture's birth (1617), but they stayed away from the threatening south shore, keeping near the relative safety of the wooden palisades of the town of Québec).

By contrast, New Netherlands, New England and New Spain were growing rapidly, with scores of new colonial towns and beyond them, thriving and expanding farming, logging and mining settlements – including the influx of British Puritans to New England in the 1630s. Thousands of colonists now called America home, including many second generation "Americans".

Guillaume may have been impatient with the rigid society into which he was born, but he was also very much a child of his era. Early 17th century France was freshly scarred from years of viscous interdenominational Wars of Religion – born out of the Protestant Reformation and the Catholic Counter-Reformation.

Unlike in the Netherlands, Britain and northern Germany, Catholicism had prevailed in that contest of religion in France, as it had in Portugal and Spain. Catholic orthodoxy was in the process of being re-established. Reformed religious orders of clergy were resurgent, including the well-educated, autonomous and disciplined Order of Jesus, the Jesuits.

Acting as both Prime Minister to the King and an ecclesiastical leader, Cardinal Richelieu and his agents imposed order and compliance throughout France. In the restive Provinces of Brittany and Normandy where Protestantism had flourished, conspicuous demonstrations of Catholic virtue were now prudent. Like many other working families in Rouen, the Couture family was earnestly Catholic, regularly attending the parish church of St-Godard.

The resurgent Catholicism of 17th century France was more benign than the ruthless conflicts of the late 16th century, despite episodes like Cardinal Richelieu's suppression of the Protestant bastion of La Rochelle. Fortunately for him, young Guillaume was exposed to some of the best of the effort to restore the vigour and acceptance of Catholicism across France. It included a focus on literacy and the education of youth, and on clerical and personal self-sacrifice.

Taking its cue from the relatively progressive rule of Henry IV and his Edict of Nantes at the turn of the century, religious tolerance was spreading in France, although born as much from civil war exhaustion and military stalemate, as from high-minded conviction. Still, tolerance helped to assuage the nominally compliant Protestants of Normandy and Brittany, allowing Norman and Breton towns to lift their focus to the expanding world beyond their provinces. In young Guillaume, as with Champlain and others, this spirit likely opened his inquiring mind to other, even more exotic faiths and customs that he would soon encounter.

Evangelism

In many European countries, this was an era featuring zealous affirmations of religious commitment – but it was also an era with a commercial impetus for exploring lucrative new markets. From the Pilgrims in New England to the Spanish conquistadors in Mexico and Peru, these two strong social currents found a happy juxtaposition in overseas evangelization, especially in America.

Admittedly, some of these well-intentioned efforts would wane or morph later in the century into activities of more dubious merit. By the 18th century, these trends would have a devastating impact on Native Americans and their societies. But these earlier, nobler sentiments imprinted themselves on the Norman and Breton generation of Guillaume's youth.

It also seems quite evident that Guillaume was not afflicted with the dogmatic, superstitious and intolerant beliefs common to sects of the era. Throughout his life, his Christianity appears to reflect his conceptual thinking and likely the influence of educated Jesuits: he saw religion as an uplifting experience for those exposed to its precepts of charity, understanding and humanity, sustained by proponents selflessly devoted to propagating those ideals.

As in past centuries in Europe, one of the few routes out of the ranks of the peasantry and the working poor in 17th century France lay through the church. 'Reformed' Catholicism was sustained and advanced by revitalized religious orders of priests and nuns, like the Récollets, the Ursulines and the Jesuits. Unable to rely on the children of the European Catholic nobility to staff their ambitious projects, these religious orders were initially, reluctantly, 'democratized'. They began recruiting talented young men and women, irrespective of their humble backgrounds, both to become clergy and to serve the clergy in their enterprises. A bright, vigourous, young carpenter who could read was an uncommon find for the Jesuits, with their fresh mandate from Richelieu to build a presence in Canada – and an informed curiosity about Champlain's New World was an added bonus.

René Goupil, a young Loire Valley surgeon eight years older than Guillaume, met Couture through the Jesuits in Rouen. Although valued as a surgeon, Goupil had been diagnosed as partially deaf and too ill to complete the long, arduous training to become a Jesuit in Paris. As a result, he signed-on with the Jesuits as a "donné" – a lay volunteer who agreed to share for a few years the hardships of the priestly missionaries, including their clerical vows of poverty, celibacy and obedience. This vocation as a donné also showed Guillaume the way out of his dead-end life as a carpenter in Rouen.

As J. G. Shaw explains, the donnés were something new for the frontier religious missions and, for that matter, for the Catholic Church. They were laymen who, without becoming clergy, bound themselves by a solemn written promise to the service of the mission with no compensation other than basic necessities. Their service in the Huron missions project went beyond the use of their labours and talents. They could also do things either forbidden to the Jesuits or impractical for them – such as carrying muskets for hunting or defense.

They also played a salutary 'marketing' role. Their largely exemplary lives provided a partial antidote to the impression left on the Natives by roving "Christian" fur traders and coureurs-de-bois, who 'led lives conformable neither to the Huron ethic nor to their own' in the words of a contemporary observer.

Still restive and unmarried at age twenty, Guillaume justified the adventure to his devout father, Guillaume senior, and to his soon to be widowed mother, Madeleine Mallet, by explaining that he, too, would be a donné. It was a higher calling than mere adventurer, and with the intervention of the Jesuits, the Coutures were persuaded to let the missionaries take their only son. Guillaume left his carpenter's bench to board one of the Jesuit-sponsored vessels making the perilous voyage to New France.

CHAPTER 2

The lessons of Tadoussac

Tadoussac

Perhaps as early as the spring of 1637, Guillaume bade adieu to his mother, sister and ailing father. He sought-out a small sailing ship commissioned by the Jesuits, in the busy little fishing port of Honfleur, across from the great harbour of Le Havre on the Seine. Ahead of him were many storm-tossed weeks on the turbulent North Atlantic, aiming to find the little all-weather anchorage of Tadoussac, a thousand uncharted leagues away.

The sea journey was typically a treacherous one. The French did not make the voyage in the grand 18th century sailing ships of film and pirate novels. They came later. These ships were very small and with imperfect navigation. In the 17th century, the crossing took an unpredictable number of weeks, navigating against prevailing westerly winds and periodic gales. As the "shortest" course was the northern Great Circle route, tracking near Iceland, Greenland and Labrador, the waves were high, the decks were slick and the rigging was often covered in ice. Sleeping was cramped and in hammocks. Food and water were often in short supply. Deaths en route from disease and misadventure were not uncommon.

Despite the courage of their decision to journey to the New World, young 'citified' apprentices – like the medical student René Goupil, the carpenter Guillaume Couture and later, a schoolteacher-seminarian also from Rouen, named René-Robert Cavelier, Sieur de LaSalle – often began their adventures in the New World as naïve or even gentle souls. The New

World would either toughen them to the arduous life of the wilderness, or drive them home. Often, the New World would exact an even greater, fatal price for their trusting innocence or their inability to adapt. Guillaume's extensive New World education would begin when the mist cleared above the spring ice-flows on the broad St. Lawrence, revealing the little dock at Tadoussac.

Today, the picturesque little village of Tadoussac is a pleasant three-hour drive down the north shore of the St. Lawrence from Québec City. In the mid-seventeenth century, however, it was an isolated outpost in the immense wilderness of North America, reached only by whalers and fishermen after a perilous sea voyage, or by fur traders and missionaries after a risky trip by canoe from the equally isolated village of Québec.

Soon after landing at Tadoussac, Guillaume encountered a local branch of the Montagnais nation, which had hunted and fished along the towering Saguenay fjord and the widening St. Lawrence River for centuries. Each spring in recent years, a number of these Natives migrated to the little settlement of Tadoussac for trade and out of curiosity. They also took comfort in the knowledge that they greatly out-numbered the French and the other traders and fishermen who took-up seasonal residence there.

Unlike their Aboriginal compatriots in New England and in the Great Lakes region, the Montagnais were an uncomplicated and generally peaceable society. Supported by a subsistence hunting-and-gathering existence, they were constantly vulnerable to the seasonal privations of a harsh environment and to raids by their Native neighbours. As a result, the Montagnais tended to see the French as a salutary counter-balance against their many threats, even if the diseases and curious attitudes of the White Man carried their own risks.

In the late spring and early summer, the Montagnais would hunt seals and whales from fragile boats and with primitive gear. In late autumn as the river froze, the Natives braved the cold to catch fish and eels for the long winter and then journeyed back into the snowy bush to trap beaver for the French. Before that winter season, during those long, slow summers and autumns in little Tadoussac, Guillaume befriended young Montagnais men of his own age.

As with all who made landfall in the all-weather port of Tadoussac, Guillaume found the mouth of the dramatic Saguenay fjord to be home to the "sea monster" great whales of boyhood stories in Normandy. He also saw many of their 'smaller' minke cousins and the pods of belugas. With instruction from the local Montagnais youths, increasingly in their own language, he mastered that most Canadian art – the art of the canoe. Together, they delighted in paddling among the whales, including the playful, white, baby-faced belugas – all still a marvel to a wide-eyed Guillaume.

Guillaume likely worked for more than one season at Tadoussac: honing his carpentry craft, and building palisades and rough-hewn homes; observing and querying the culture and practices of the Montagnais, including the craft of the canoe; and, learning new skills from the local French traders and soldiers, including musketry and the arcane skills needed to fire an arquebus. He grew to love this new land – ripe with possibilities and adventure.

The Canoe and the Musket

The canoe was a marvelous discovery for Guillaume. Fashioned from the smooth, white bark of the birch, it was woven together over a skeleton of sturdy fir branches with the sinews of spruce roots. Easily carried by two men, it moved through cold streams and choppy lakes with a silent, steady pulse that outdistanced any human or animal pace. While European vessels might be careened for weeks when damaged on rocks or from cargo, a freight canoe could be repaired within forty-eight hours by patches fused from readily accessible animal fat and pine tar. Guillaume's carpentry skills morphed easily into framing canoes and weaving them watertight with binding twine stretched from the sinewy roots of fir trees.

A special treat was to paddle and climb to the vantage point of Cap-Trinité, where rivulets cascaded out of the cliffs and down the sheer south face of the majestic Saguenay fjord. From there, with his Montagnais companions, Guillaume could watch the wide Saguenay river flow to the salty St. Lawrence, with wispy smoke from the wood fires of the French settlement and the Native encampments in the distance.

From the village dock, he observed the water-borne trade with little Tadoussac – cod-fishing, whaling and supply vessels from Europe, and perhaps more intriguingly the long, fur-laden canoes from deep in the unknown interior which fed the rivers of the Saguenay, the St. Lawrence, the Richelieu and the Ottawa.

Over time, Guillaume's growing skill with a musket made him a popular addition to Montagnais hunting parties foraging around Tadoussac. Unlike the English and the Dutch, the French would not trade weapons for furs, so including a Frenchman in the hunting party was a better guarantee of success against an empty winter larder. These forays did not just improve Guillaume's musketry, and the physical robustness and endurance of a "city kid". They opened the door to learning from his companions the ways of the forest and the forest animals that were the subsistence diet and source of livelihood of the Montagnais and their Native compatriots.

This unhurried time also allowed Guillaume to observe Native lifestyles, practices, and folk-culture outside of the formal and suspicious interactions that often characterized Native dealings with European traders, officials and clergy. From the masters, he learned how to thrive in the bush – way-finding, canoe repair, trapping and game-tracking – but also picking-up essential little tricks for enduring those equally daunting Canadian forest scourges: the cold, the wet, the snow and ice, and of course, the mosquito and the vicious little black-fly.

Beginning to understand the Iroquois

Like Champlain, Guillaume came to respect and to treat as equals his Aboriginal companions, from whom he learned much that was useful and much that dispelled prevailing European cultural and religious prejudices. Perhaps unlike Champlain, he learned early that there were important differences among the Native nations – who were as different from one another as Spaniards were from the Dutch. In particular, Guillaume came to know and to fear – by reputation, from both French and Native sources – the Iroquois.

Guillaume knew that the French and their Native allies lived in constant fear of the war parties of the legendary Five Nations of the Iroquois Confederacy. The ascendant Native power of eastern North America, the Iroquois nations – at that time the nations of the Mohawk, Onondaga, Oneida, Cayuga and Seneca – were expanding their influence and their control of trade across a wide territory, ultimately extending from present-day Ohio to New England, and from Pennsylvania to the interior of today's provinces of Ontario and Québec. Later this aggressive Confederacy would project its influence and suppression campaigns as far as Illinois, Wisconsin and into Sioux territory.

Growing from several neighbouring and often contending tribes, by the beginning of the 17th century, the few hundred warriors of the Mohawks had persuaded their Iroquois cousins, with the exception of the linguistically related Huron nations, to join a 'confederacy'. The Iroquois were ruled by a complex governance structure – the Great Law of Peace (*Gayanashagowa*), with over 100 detailed, orally preserved precepts. It revolved around the symbolism of the longhouse (the Haudenosaunee) and its intricacy and balance impressed all who studied it, including evidently Benjamin Franklin and James Madison. The Iroquois had prospered over the subsequent four decades with a belligerent culture of raiding parties and seizing captives, increasingly bolstered by being the only major Native group with liberal access to firearms.

Like the Prussians forging Germany in the 19th century, and with much the same ethos and attitude towards their "neighbours", the Mohawks welded the Iroquois into a potent, aggressive confederacy. Anthropologists differ about the time frame for the Confederacy and its Great Law. Some say the confederacy began as early as the 13th century, while others have it as late as the mid-16th century. The legends of the Peacemaker, himself an outsider from the Bay of Quinte area of present-day Ontario, and his eloquent spokesman, Hiawatha (a name later 'borrowed' for Longfellow's heroine), surround the development of the Great Law and the Confederacy.

Regardless of the date of the Confederacy's origin and despite the alluring promise of unified action, things did not go well for the Iroquois in its early centuries. Until the turn of the 17th century, the Iroquois were a beleaguered collection of tribes evicted by the Mi'Kmaq and the Algonquin, including the Mohicans, from most of New England, the lower St. Lawrence valley and Gulf of St. Lawrence. In the century between Cartier's first encounter with Iroquoians along the St. Lawrence in 1535 and Champlain's arrival in New France in 1608, they had been pushed south and west into contemporary New York State.

By the time of Champlain's arrival, however, an Iroquois resurgence was underway. Collective action, forged in the face of adversity, had welded the Iroquois into a potent Native state. Like the German Empire in 19th century Europe, the Iroquois found themselves at a geographical crossroads in Upstate New York and the upper St. Lawrence valley – surrounded and legitimately fearful of constant encroachment. Always shrewd and enterprising, they turned their location from a liability into an asset. The Confederacy took full advantage of its linchpin geographic position, its culture of survival-based, wide-ranging belligerence and raiding, and its pluralistic collection of nations and clans.

The Iroquois' thriving economy and prosperous "castle" towns supplemented the spoils from raiding neighbouring tribes with productive domestic agriculture, hunting and fishing. Its decision-making structure reflected a 'federal' approach, balancing a capacity for concerted action, against an unwillingness to bind the confederacy's autonomous 'national' and 'clan' partners against their will. Its culture valued reasoned rhetoric, bravery, loyalty and pluralism, in themselves and others. Its culture also distained weakness, exploited leveraging advantage, and despite its accommodation and adoption of conquered foes, it harbored a long-lived and vigorous taste for retribution for those who had the temerity to resist.

By the mid-1600s, the Iroquois became a fearsome entity, for both Aboriginals and Europeans alike. (It is no accident that New Englanders selected the garb of "Mohawks" to instill fear in the British at the Boston Tea Party).

The Iroquois' prosperity and success in combat produced a society that was able to move beyond the subsistence hunting-and-gathering economic model of their neighbours and their ancestors. Over time, the Iroquois accumulated the resources to build permanent fortified towns, fed by extensive, cultivated field crops, and to control intermediary trade in furs and other trade goods over a wide area. Although warlike and aggressive, the Iroquois did not wage war or acquire and hold territory in the fashion of Europeans, or their distant cousins the Aztecs and the Incas. The Iroquois were generally wide-ranging raiders and skirmishers – they used their military power to enrich themselves, to control trade routes, and to dominate their Aboriginal neighbours, subjugating them to their interests. A unique feature was their propensity to capture and adopt prisoners, and even to incorporate entire defeated tribes into their society, which continually expanded in numbers as a result.

The Hurons and the Iroquois – and the French

The Iroquois Confederacy's relationship with the Hurons, however, was different in character. Like the Iroquois, the five tribes or nations of the Huron had come together in a confederacy, dominated by the Arendarhonon nation on the northern reaches of the Huron homeland between Lake Huron's Georgian Bay and Lake Simcoe. Also like the Iroquois, the Huron were a more advanced Native society, with fortified villages of longhouses, surrounded by field crops. They developed and dominated trading relations with the Indian nations to their north and east – the tribes of the Anishinabeck (Ojibwa, Ottawa and Algonquin) and the Cree. In the eyes of the Iroquois, their linguistic cousins, the Hurons may have been a prospective or inevitable addition to the Iroquois Confederacy at the turn of the 17th century, much as they later welcomed the sixth nation, the Iroquoian Tuscarora from Carolina in the early 18th century.

Then, in 1609, Champlain fatefully and almost accidentally tipped the political and military balance across east-central North America. Early in the tenuous settlement of New France, Champlain was persuaded by his new ally, preeminent Chief Atironta, to side with the Hurons in a few minor skirmishes with the Iroquois. Suddenly, the Hurons went from 'poor cousin' in the wider Iroquoian family to privileged trading partner with one of the most reliable and generous of European allies, the French. By demonstrating the terrifying effect of 'fire sticks' on Iroquois war parties that had not yet encountered them, the French and the Hurons immediately created a relentless demand for firearms by the Iroquois in their century-long trade dealings with the Dutch and the English. These events also made the French and the Huron the merciless enemy of a powerful and ascendant group of Indian Nations for a century.

Before long, the Iroquois were well equipped with Dutch and later British firearms and bitterly determined to reduce the Huron and to destroy the French. Or perhaps in keeping with an Iroquois strategy that had served them well elsewhere, to harass the French until they accepted the Iroquois as their primary trade intermediaries. Throughout the early decades of the 1600s, the Iroquois returned to the St. Lawrence and Ottawa valleys, where Cartier had encountered them a century earlier. Along the hundreds of kilometers of the south shore of the St. Lawrence River and throughout the lower Great Lakes, Iroquois hunting parties and bands of warriors made life dangerous and often short for all non-Iroquois, whether French, Huron, Ojibway, Algonquin or even Montagnais or Cree.

Despite the risks, Guillaume's imagination was excited by the prospect of traversing the wilderness, and perhaps encountering these dreaded adversaries of his French and Aboriginal friends.

THE NEW WORLD OF GUILLAUME COUTURE

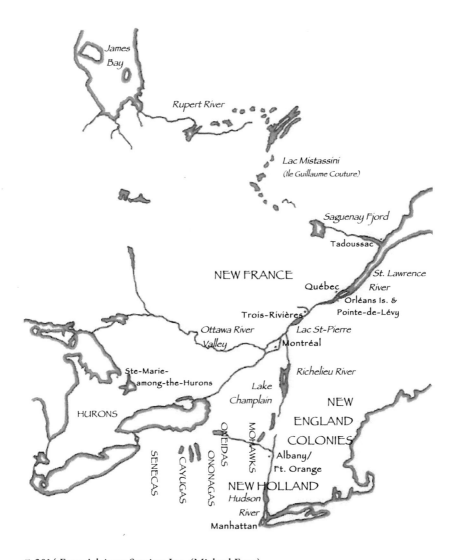

James Bay

Rupert River

Lac Mistassini
(Ile Guillaume Couture)

Saguenay Fjord

Tadoussac

NEW FRANCE

Québec

St. Lawrence River

Orléans Is. &
Pointe-de-Lévy

Trois-Rivières

Lac St-Pierre

Ottawa River Valley

Montréal

Ste-Marie-among-the-Hurons

Richelieu River

Lake Champlain

NEW ENGLAND COLONIES

HURONS

SENECAS

CAYUGAS

ONONAGAS

ONEIDAS

MOHAWKS

Albany/ Ft. Orange

NEW HOLLAND

Hudson River

Manhattan

© 2014 Fenn Advisory Services Inc. (Michael Fenn)

CHAPTER 3

Navigating a trackless wilderness

Bringing Christianity to the peoples of the New World

A key element of French policy was evangelization. It was a matter of duty and also a sensitive point with the conspicuously Catholic French monarchy. Champlain and others, including nobles closely associated with the clergy, used that 'Christianization of the heathen' imperative to secure funding for early 17th century ventures that often had more to do with European settlement and trade, especially the lucrative fur trade.

Once successful in securing royal support, however, the corollary was a need to seek-out the Native peoples where they lived. Many lives were lost to misadventure and martyrdom, as Catholic religious orders like the Récollets and the Jesuits went on missions through the trackless wilderness. Others, such as Étienne Brûlé, were lost to the lure of life among the Natives.

In the early 17th century, Cardinal Richelieu looked to a Catholic religious order – the Society of Jesus or Jesuits – to re-mount France's efforts in North America. Aptly nicknamed "God's soldiers", their success in helping the Catholic Church hold back the tide of the Protestant Reformation owed a lot to their paramilitary organization, their extensive education (8-13 years of advanced study) and their ascetic, determined focus. Evangelizing the reluctant Native nations of North America, while earning the support of European nobility and the Papacy, was the kind of assignment they relished.

The Jesuits analyzed the failed past efforts by the French to convert the Native peoples of northeastern North America to Christianity, which had proved costly, dangerous and usually ephemeral. Despite this, French trade and trade goods were very welcome by Natives. In fact, for the Natives, the French were a valuable counterbalance to the Dutch and British trading partners of their enemies, the Iroquois.

Efforts to go beyond trade and to convert Natives to Christianity, on those occasions when the Natives' fur-trading flotillas visited New France, were quickly eroded by traditional shamans when they returned to their home villages. Itinerant visits to Native villages by priests were equally unsuccessful. In fact, the periodic visits by the French clergy seemed to coincide with the outbreak of contagious illness, which shamans were quick (and ironically, correct) to link to the Black Robes – clear evidence that the traditional gods were not pleased.

It became clear to the Jesuits that the French would need to sink roots in the midst of the homelands of the Native peoples, particularly among the less nomadic nations like the Hurons and the Iroquois, if they were ever going to enjoy any sustainable success with their evangelization efforts. For a New France colony huddled precariously in palisaded enclaves on the north shore of the St. Lawrence River, moving a thousand leagues west into the forests of the Great Lakes basin was easily said, but not easily accomplished. The resolute belligerence of the omnipresent Iroquois only added to the challenge and the risks. But that was the approach the Jesuits had taken in India, China and South America, with considerable success, so they determined to repeat the strategy.

To succeed in this daring venture, the Jesuits knew that they would need more than brave priests. They would need a unique type of person to support their venture. They would need brave young men who shared their lofty objectives and their ethical code of self-denial, rather than just seeing the venture as a privileged entrée into an undeniably lucrative source of valuable furs. They would need men who knew the ways of the woods like a Native, but who could bring to bear very European skills like carpentry and musketry. They would need hardy, experienced oarsmen and navigators to face the many treacherous rivers, rapids and portages stretching across the vast distance back to Québec. Above all, they would need men who could speak the languages and understand the customs of those they were aiming to convert. It was a rare and challenging job description, especially when they added vows of poverty, obedience and chastity to the formal contract engaging their "donnés".

It is no surprise, then, that Guillaume was enthusiastically welcomed when he volunteered to be part of the initial party of eighteen Frenchmen, setting-out for Huron country in late 1639.

Ste-Marie-among-the-Hurons

With characteristic élan, the Jesuits did not select a site for their pioneering settlement on the edge of the wilderness. Rather they chose a site in the midst of the largest and most powerful of the Huron clans and shamans, simultaneously recognizing the preeminence of the Hurons in relation to all of their neighbours, save for the implacable Iroquois.

Father Jérôme Lalemant, who became the second superior of the Jesuit mission in the land of the Hurons in 1638 and was later to be canonized as a saint and martyr, described in the *Jesuit Relations* the central location chosen in the Huron-Wendat territory on the shore of a beautiful little river, and the merits of his settlement plan:

> *"[...] And thus we have now in all the country but a single house which is to be firm and stable, — the vicinity of the waters being very advantageous to us for supplying the want, in these regions, of every other vehicle; and the lands being fairly good for the native corn, which we intend, as time goes on, to harvest for ourselves."*[1]

After thirty days of non-stop canoeing, up the churning Ottawa and Mattawa rivers, and then traversing Lake Nipissing and the rapids and falls of the French River and across storm-tossed Georgian Bay in Lake Huron, they arrived at the mouth of the Wye River in November 1639. The priests and their lay workers, including Guillaume, erected a makeshift shelter out of cypress pillars and a birch bark roof, using clay to build in the interior walls. Initially, it was the most they could do to defend themselves against the perils of the impending winter and the prospect of Iroquois raiding parties. Through the autumn of 1639 and the winter of 1640, Guillaume and the other Frenchmen with requisite skills erected the first dwelling in the rudimentary "en piliers" or post style.

That first year at Ste-Marie Guillaume met and worked along side Father Isaac Jogues, with whom he would subsequently share many harrowing weeks in the Mohawk River valley. Among the donnés, in addition to Guillaume, there was Joseph Mollere, a pharmacist, Robert Le Coq, who was listed as "buyer" or "chief of supply", and Christopher Regnault, the shoemaker who later left a vivid account of the martyrdoms of Brébeuf and Lalemant.

The "adolescents" mentioned below by Lalemant were apparently young men of twelve to sixteen years of age serving a probation to become donnés, as the two did by 1643, or learning the Huron language so as later to engage in the fur trade. One of them was Pierre Boucher, a notable figure in the history of New France and future Governor of the Trois-Rivières district of New France.

In the spring of 1640, carpenter Charles Boivin arrived to bolster and guide their efforts. Along with his illustrious, church-building brother François, Charles had learned skills that went beyond carpentry to rudimentary architecture. A young contemporary of Guillaume in the Rouen carpentry guild, Charles put the woodworking skills of Guillaume to best advantage. With Guillaume and others explaining the requirements, in their own language, to their Native co-workers – the French tradesmen erected a chapel, a residence for the Jesuit priests, a cookhouse, a smithy and other buildings, including a rudimentary carpentry shop. In the following decade, Ste-Marie became a small village of two-dozen buildings, boasting a blacksmith's shop, two churches, a refectory, a hospital, several workshops, a number of cultivated fields and a stable.

Present-day visitors to the Ste-Marie-among-the-Hurons restoration, near Midland in Ontario, will see a "living museum" replica site that illustrates the achievements of Guillaume and his colleagues at the height of Ste-Marie's development, even down to the detail of an actor playing a young carpenter named "Guillaume".

At a time when a recently restored French colony of Québec had dipped to a European population numbering in the dozens, Ste-Marie was well established as the first permanent European settlement west of Montréal, in the vast territory between the English forts on Hudson Bay and the Hudson River Dutch settlements at Albany and Manhattan. Ste-Marie had become the Jesuit headquarters in Huronia, from which the Jesuits travelled among the Huron, Petun, Nipissing, Ottawa and Ojibway peoples.

J. G. Shaw describes the progress in his description of early Ste-Marie: By the autumn of 1640 Father Lalemant could draw up a *"catalogus personarum"* that satisfied even his passion for organization. There were twenty-eight names and all were categorized according to their assignments. Among the thirteen priests, Father Jean de Brébeuf was listed as "Advisor to the superior, spiritual director, in charge of the chapel and one of two confessors for the Jesuits". One lay brother, Dominic Scot (probably of Irish or Scottish origin), appears as "tailor". The lay staff consisted of six "donnés", two "adolescents", two "boys", and four "workmen, not donnés".

In our contemporary world, parents are likely appalled at the prospect of sending youngsters to live away from family in such dangerous circumstances, with the attendant risk of injury, abuse and even death. But evidently the opportunities afforded by such an experience outweighed these concerns. The record of those who "graduated" from this experience – fluent in Native languages and life-saving wilderness skills – tends to confirm this view. Still, it seems to be cold-hearted and uncaring treatment of children by our standards and evidence of the harshness of life, and life's choices, on the frontier.

A friend returns

In 1640, as the ice in the upper reaches of the St. Lawrence began spring break-up, a long-anticipated supply ship arrived in Québec, via Tadoussac, from France. On the deck was Guillaume's friend and early inspiration René Goupil. After several seasons in the tiny outpost, the younger Guillaume was an experienced hand among the population of New France. Goupil, the surgeon and newcomer, would be expected to serve the Native converts in the mission station of Sillery, near the little settlement of Québec.

Both Couture and Goupil would have shared the same experience, coming up-river from Tadoussac. As their little vessel rounded Orléans Island in the middle of the river channel, they saw Québec's wooden ramparts rise on their right. Perched high on the cliffs overlooking dangerous Lévis Point on the opposite shore, Québec maintained a watchful defense against the recurrent threat from Iroquois war parties on the south shore and up-river, not forgetting the recently departed New England privateers from down-river. In the spring of 1640, the village of Québec was coming to life after many months of being sealed-off from the world by the ice-bound St. Lawrence and the deep snow of the 'impenetrable' wilderness. New France looked optimistically, as it always did, to a better year than the last.

While René Goupil was commissioned by the Jesuits to work for two years (1640-42) as a surgeon in the Sillery mission, Guillaume experienced the adventure of living and working in the trackless wilds of the interior of America.

After his initial voyage in late 1639 to Ste-Marie, Guillaume made a series of month-long canoe trips across Lake Huron's wind-swept Georgian Bay, up the French River and Lake Nipissing and then down the roiling Ottawa River to the St. Lawrence at present-day Montréal, and on to Trois-Rivières.

On the thirty-day trip, their days and nights were filled with plagues of tiny, blood-drawing blackflies and swarms of mosquitoes, and while resting, the cracking forest noises that might betray a bear or wolves, or an Iroquois raiding party. The punishing daily grind of constant paddling and arduous portaging through the trackless bush had few respites. Only the rhythmic songs that paced the paddlers – "call-and-response" songs – and the relief of fresh fish over a smoky fire offered any comfort. An exhausted sleep on pine boughs was shallow and one-eye-open, against the ever-present threat of the Mohawks and their allies.

After a brief respite, Guillaume and his compatriots repeated the return journey upstream. At the end of a month of non-stop daily paddling, they reached the little palisaded European outpost in the heart of Huron-Wendat country, a land stretching from Lake Huron to Lake Simcoe, which the Hurons called Wendake and we now call Huronia.

The outpost was designed to teach the Natives of the religion of the French; but it did much to teach the French, if they were open to it. They saw that they would benefit from learning and adopting the traditional wisdom of the Iroquoian Hurons, as well as their language and culture.

Some proved excellent 'students'. In 1641, for example, Guillaume and his compatriots welcomed a new Ste-Marie resident, recently arrived from the Normandy coast port of Dieppe. Charles Le Moyne was nine years younger than Guillaume, so the older Frenchmen were careful to caution him of the risks and realities of life in the wilderness. He learned well and stayed for four years. Like Guillaume, Charles used this experience as the foundation for a remarkable life in the New World, a true pioneer.

Following his tenure at Ste-Marie, Le Moyne settled in the fledgling St. Lawrence River outpost of Trois-Rivières, as an interpreter, clerk and militiaman. When the call went out for volunteers to build Ville-Marie (Montréal), at the dangerous western limits of established New France, Le Moyne joined up. A pioneer of Montréal, where he lived until his death in February 1685, Charles is likely better remembered for the exploits of many of his fourteen, Montréal-born children. Some of them are remembered for the founding of Louisiana, including Biloxi (Mississippi), Mobile (Alabama) and New Orleans, as well as their battles with the English and the Iroquois, including raids on the English forts on Hudson Bay and the notorious Schenectady (New Netherlands) reprisal massacre, commemorated annually to this day by that City's Mayor.

The donné's (temporary) pledge: a vow of poverty, chastity and obedience

A document with Guillaume's signature comes down to us, dated the 26th of June 1641. It looks a lot like a Last Will and Testament, so one wonders if he anticipated the worst on his first major forays into the bush. In fact, as a donné, Guillaume knew that the Jesuits took seriously their expectations that donnés would share their vows of chastity, obedience, and poverty. The twin temptations of the flesh and of the profits from the fur-trade were ever-present among the French couriers-du-bois ('woods-runners'), and the Jesuits expected young Guillaume to foreswear both.

As result, Guillaume apparently decided to make a very public attestation of his status by preparing a document that he had notarized by Martial Piraubé and filed at Québec, before his first journey to Ste-Marie-among-the-Hurons.

In that document, Guillaume assigned his 'goods' and his power of attorney to his sister and his mother, although his uncle Victore Cousture, a labourer at La Haye-Aubrey in Normandy, was technically his guardian. At the same time, he deeded over a small parcel of land in the parish of La Haye-Aubray (also now spelled Aubrey and Aubrée). The parcel had been left to Guillaume by his late father, so with this renunciation, he was now technically without any assets or wealth, meeting the Jesuit's test of 'poverty'. As for his vows of celibacy and obedience, they would be put to more practical tests in the wilderness.

Signing as a 'servant of the Reverend Fathers of the Society of Jesus in the Huron mission in New France', Guillaume spells his name 'Cousture'. The spelling seems to have evolved later to 'Coûture', first with a 'chapeau' indicating the 'dropping' of an 's', and later dropping it entirely, as 'Couture' came to be common North American usage in subsequent centuries. In Old French, "cousture" implied sewing grain, but later as "couture", came to be associated with sewing of garments (and in our day, fashion). This evolution was to have a curious repetition for Couture as he encountered the Iroquois.

From Ste-Marie-among-the-Hurons to Québec – thirty days by canoe

In addition to the ever-present threat of ambush by the Iroquois and the great physical exertion involved, the canoe trip itself from Québec to Ste-Marie was a naturally dangerous voyage. Guillaume learned, for example, that the Récollet Falls on the French River were not named as an honour to that religious order, but after the unfortunate Récollet priests who had fatally failed to hear the crashing water ahead of them, before hurtling over the cascade in their canoe. With Lake Nipissing as headwater to both the French River and Mattawa / Ottawa rivers, this canoe route also had the unenviable distinction of including a 600 kilometre (400 mile) paddle against an often raging current, in both directions!

The portage-filled voyage with heavy canoes and back-bending supply packs covered some 1280 kilometers (800 miles) but Guillaume and his Native and French colleagues averaged a remarkable 40 kilometres (25 miles) per day. Guillaume and his compatriots certainly earned the French sobriquet "voyageur". Among the things brought from Québec were heavy items that added to portaging's back-bending trial. The awls, blades, saws, iron axes and planes needed to turn Boivin's designs for Ste-Marie into reality had to be transported by canoe under very difficult conditions, by very fit young men. Cutting-down old growth forest to produce planed lumber and finished European-style wood-framing was arduous work that began with transporting the implements to make it possible.

In the winter of 1641-42, with ice closing the canoe routes, Guillaume over-wintered again at Ste-Marie with the missionaries, his fellow countrymen and their Huron Christian converts, doing construction and carpentry, hunting and reading, and continuing to learn the complex Iroquoian language of the Huron Wendat. In the spring of 1642, Guillaume was asked to join a large travel party, in four long freight canoes, returning to Québec. Among the two-dozen members of the party were several notables.

Acclaimed Huron Chief and warrior Ahatsistari, who had recently been baptized as "Eustache", had led two of the most successful 1641 Huron attacks on the Seneca nation of the Iroquois Confederacy (after the 1634 peace treaty with the Iroquois was breached by the Hurons, in 1639). Despite his recent conversion to Christianity, the Iroquois could not rely on "Eustache" to embrace its precepts of mercy and brotherly love. Ahatsistari was a name that struck fear in the hearts of the Iroquois, and his capture would be a major coup.

Also in the company was legendary Jesuit Father Isaac Jogues, who had established the Jesuits' tenuous but persistent presence in the Huron country (present-day western Ontario) in 1634 and who had lived there since that time. Finally, the party included another Jesuit, Father Charles Raymbault (also spelled Raymbaut), whose failing health and past administrative experience meant he would be more useful to the Jesuits back in Québec.

The party left Ste-Marie in Huronia on June 13, 1642. Despite Father Jogues's written accounts of forty portages around rapids and waterfalls, they made the perilous journey in a remarkable thirty-five days, without capsizings and without encountering the Iroquois. In spite of his once robust physique and extensive journeys in the west country, or perhaps because of the toll they exacted, Father Raymbault's health continued to decline after being delivered safely to Québec. Unable to return to health, he died at the age of forty, on October 22nd and was buried next to Champlain, in a location no longer known to us.

For his part, Guillaume's first seasons of adventure were now behind him, but another was about to begin. After briefly enjoying the meager civilized amenities of the village of Québec for two weeks, and after the Jesuits observed the feast day of their founder, Ignatius Loyola on July 31, the party from the Huron country was again preparing to return to Ste-Marie-among-the-Hurons at the beginning of August 1642. Having completed his business with the French, Ahatsistari was also eager to return home. With him on the return voyage would be Huron leader and ardent Christian convert "Joseph" Teondechoren, who would be bringing back from Québec his slain brother's daughter, fourteen-year old student of the Ursulines, "Thérèse" Oionhaton.

Another member of the party would be Guillaume's friend from Rouen and fellow donné, René Goupil.

(1)   From: Reuben Gold Thwaites (ed.), *The Jesuit Relations and Allied Documents: Travels and Explorations of the Jesuit Missionaries in New France 1610-1791*, Burrows Brothers Company, Publishers (Cleveland OH: 1898); see ***Bibliography***

CHAPTER 4

A battle in the woods

A perilous journey

Departing on August 1, 1642, Guillaume, Father Isaac Jogues, René Goupil, "Eustache" Ahatsistari, "Thérèse" Oionhaton, "Joseph" Teondechoren, an unidentified French labourer destined for Ste-Marie, and thirty-three Huron warriors began paddling a dozen light canoes up the narrowing St. Lawrence, heading into the foreboding upriver country between New France and Huronia. On August 2nd, they paddled past the last tenuous, western outpost of New France at Trois-Rivières and made landfall where the St. Lawrence widens briefly to form Lac St-Pierre.

Many of the exploits of early Europeans in America are lost in the misty past of legend and memory. In this case, however, we have a remarkably thorough and accurate account of subsequent events. In common with other adventures of the age in New France, all were dutifully recorded by the erudite Jesuits who survived. Beginning in 1632 and for a generation thereafter, experiences and observations about the new world were carefully chronicled for the Jesuit "mother house" in Paris, in the form of the annual installments of the Jesuit *Relations*.

While the French were wary of the watery path ahead, they took comfort in the leadership of Ahatsistari. He had met the Iroquois in battle and had beaten them largely through courage and skill, both on water and on land. In fact, the Jesuits recount that, on the sides of the Hurons' canoes "flapping in the wind like fluff-balls" were the scalps of dead enemies, including prisoners. More sober travelers might have reflected that such demonstrations of lack of mercy might find themselves reciprocated, if the tables were turned.

The flotilla threaded the islands at the southern end of Lac St-Pierre, hoping to screen their movements from the eyes of any Iroquois scouts. They selected a good encampment; a thickly wooded shoreline camouflaged by tall reeds, and set-up an unfortified camp for the night.

By now, they were well into Iroquois country, and they knew it. To add to their feeling of unease, the lead canoe of Huron scouts discovered footprints in the soft mud nearby. Some took comfort in the assumption that they might be allied Algonquins. Others suspected they were evidence of an Iroquois war party. Ahatsistari was disdainful of such fears.

"Whether they be friend or foe, doesn't matter – from their tracks I can tell that they are not as numerous as us," he boasted, according to Jesuit accounts. *"Let us advance and not worry about anything".* His experience and bravado won the day, and the group began to make camp.[(2)]

While he admired Ahatsistari's courage, the canny Guillaume evidently was not persuaded that the Iroquois posed no serious threat. The canoes that were their only practical escape could easily be damaged, as they lay unprotected on the unguarded shore. The only escape would be the forest. With an illustration of his innate appreciation of strategy and tactics, he prudently took-up a position near the edge of the woods, for refuge or cover in the event of an attack during the night.

Ambush

As dawn broke over Lac St-Pierre, the reeds that were to provide protection suddenly parted. From the adjacent marsh, a flotilla of war canoes raced toward the sleeping encampment. Leaping onto the shore with heart-stopping war cries and in full war paint, Mohawks fell on the unprepared Hurons. With a thunderous roar and an acrid cloud of gunpowder smoke, the Iroquois demonstrated that they knew how to fire – but not aim – the guns the Dutch had given them. Despite the bellicose display and gunfire, little damage was done to the canoes and only one Huron received a hand injury. Three Hurons who turned to face the foe, however, were killed on the spot, in the traditional way, by tomahawk. In the confusion of dawn mist, noise and smoke, the Hurons had seen enough and ran into the woods for safety.

Amidst the screaming, confusion and tumult, the well-located Guillaume grabbed his musket and along with Father Jogues and a few others, successfully evaded the ambush. Guillaume secreted himself in the nearby undergrowth, moving surreptitiously farther into the wood as the circumstances permitted. Relieved by knowing that Father Jogues and others had made good their escape, Guillaume moved quickly through the brush and beyond earshot of the Iroquois attackers.

In a few moments, the surprised Hurons realized that there had only been a dozen or so Iroquois attackers. The Hurons rallied and counter-attacked. Before they could overcome the initial attackers, however, the Iroquois sprung the trap. The Hurons suddenly realized that the Iroquois were being reinforced – by some forty more warriors from the opposite bank. Outnumbered, out-flanked, poorly armed and chased-down by superior numbers, twenty-two Hurons surrendered or were captured trying to make their escape.

Eventually, both Goupil and Ahatsistari were also captured. Selflessly, Father Jogues decided he could not abandon his Indian converts and René Goupil. He surrendered himself to a group of Mohawk warriors who were scouring the forest for escapees.

From his vantage point at the edge of the woods with the remaining fleeing Hurons, Guillaume saw the situation unfold. He came to realize that Goupil and Jogues were captive.

At that point, the Jesuit *Relations* recount, Guillaume made the courageous decision to leave the safety of the party of fleeing Hurons and to return to share the fate of his countrymen and fellow Christians. While courageous, it was not a decision easily carried-out in the heat of battle or explained to a foe who could not understand you. Making the selfless decision to surrender unnecessarily was only part of the problem: surrendering without being killed was another.

Skirmish

Encouraged by the capture of some of those who had evaded the original ambush, one of the Mohawks' leading captains rallied his fellow warriors to continue the search for escaped enemies, with the goal of killing or capturing whomever they uncovered. As an esteemed chieftain, he carried one of the precious guns that the Mohawks had secured from the Dutch. Leading a party of four trusted warriors, he set out to flush more enemies from the nearby woods.

It was Guillaume's misfortune to decide to return to the encampment along the same forest path that this little Mohawk war party was using. As he rounded a bend into a clearing, Guillaume heard the warriors' footfalls in the snapping underbrush. He calculated that he could keep a handful of warriors at bay with his musket, if he had them before him at some distance and with a clear shot. In the worst case, he imagined that he could out-run a little war party that was likely nursing both stiff muscles from days of canoeing, as well as justified fears about wandering too far from their companions in unknown territory.

Making himself known in a loud voice, Guillaume awaited their verbal reply. What he received was more ominous – a chorus of war-hoops and the glistening dawn sunlight on the muzzle of a musket aimed at him by the warrior chieftain. An instant later, he would hear the metallic click of iron on flint.

Guillaume's short life flashed before his eyes.

While the Dutch traded guns for furs without apparent ethical concerns, their culpability did not extend to ensuring that their Iroquois customers were fully proficient in the use of firearms.

The gun misfired.

Guillaume faced a dilemma. He was willing to risk surrender. But he was not willing to sacrifice his life simply for the campfire boasting of a Mohawk chieftain. After several seasons of shooting moose and deer with the Montagnais and Hurons, Guillaume was adept with a musket – and he could not await a reloading by the Iroquois.

Guillaume's growing skill with the musket would be put to the test in the seeming eternity of a momentary confrontation: as the Mohawk aimed and misfired, an instant later Guillaume's musket ball shattered the Mohawk's chest and he collapse to the ground.

The ordeal begins

His single-shot musket had done its damage and saved his life, but it left the young Frenchman defenseless in the face four Mohawk warriors. Enraged at the loss of their comrade and leader, they wrestled Guillaume to the ground and beat him savagely with cudgels in revenge – the first of many such beatings.

Guillaume learned later that the Iroquois he had killed was a warrior of considerable clan importance. The Jesuit *Relations* recount that Guillaume was stripped, beaten with clubs, scratched with fingernails and had his fingers gnawed with their teeth. His right hand was also gashed with a knife. They then bound him by the neck and led him back to the encampment.

When Guillaume emerged from the woods as a prisoner, Father Jogues broke free of his own captors, embraced Couture and urged him to show courage. In the first of many cultural miscues that were to plague the Jesuits in captivity, the Iroquois misunderstood and thought that Guillaume was being praised for slaying a prominent Iroquois. The reaction was to inflict on Guillaume, a further, more savage beating, ultimately leaving him near death on the shore of Lac St-Pierre.

The Jesuit *Relations* recount Isaac Jogues's version of these events:

> "...*There was finally led in among the captives...Guillaume Couture, who had come with me from the Huron country. This man, seeing the impossibility of longer defending himself, had fled with the others into the forests; and as he was a young man not only of courageous disposition but strong in body and fleet in running, he was already out of the grasp of the one who was pursuing him. But having turned back and seeing that I was not with him, "I will not forsake," he said to himself, "my dear Father alone in the hands of enemies." And immediately returning to the Barbarians, he had of his own accord become a prisoner.*
>
> "*Oh, that he had never taken such a resolution! It is no consolation in such cases to have companions of one's misfortunes. But who can prevent the sentiment of charity? Such is the feeling toward us of those laymen who, without any worldly interest, serve God and aid us in our ministrations among the Hurons. This one had*

slain, in the fight, one of the most prominent among the enemies; he was therefore treated most cruelly. They stripped him naked, tore off his nails with their teeth, bit his fingers, and pierced his right hand with a javelin; but he suffered it all with such invincible patience -- remembering the nails of the Savior, as he told me afterward. I embraced him with great affection and exhorted him to offer to God those pains, for himself and for those who tormented him... "[3]

Ritual torture of captives was an accepted part of the culture of warfare among eastern North American tribes. It allowed captives to demonstrate their silent or even sung courage and it gave the victors the satisfaction of demonstrating their power and strength. "Worthy adversaries" – like Couture who killed a prominent war chief, and particularly like Ahatsistari, the Huron leader – merited especially ferocious attention. The ordeal had just begun for Guillaume and his fellow captives.

As he recovered consciousness, the remaining members of the Iroquois party tore out Guillaume's fingernails with their teeth. Next they laid bare the flesh of his index fingers, grinding them between stones to produce the maximum agony. Nearby, René Goupil received the same merciless regime of torture.

After a futile effort to capture the remaining Hurons, the Iroquois packed-up the twenty-bundle baggage of the French and Hurons as spoils of war, using their captives as bearers. Then they began the arduous thirteen-day trek back into Iroquois country (now upstate New York), not always in the "comfort" of canoes, but frequently walking like pack-mules bearing the sturdier but heavier, long-distance Iroquois-style canoes and loot over rugged forest tracks and rocky portages.

By mid-August 1642, Guillaume and his beleaguered colleagues disappear from the knowledge of New France and are presumed dead. Soon, the captured Frenchmen were given a further reason to despair of their future. Their little southbound coterie of warriors and captives encountered a 200-member hunting party of Iroquois braves. While game was their goal, their numbers and range meant that this northbound party was ready to mete-out a similar fate to any French, Huron or Algonquin they encountered along the south side of the St. Lawrence valley. It was a disillusioning prospect for the little, poorly defended settlements of

Québec, Trois-Rivières and the proposed post on the island one day to be occupied by Montréal.

Despite the reasonable fears of those in Québec in the ensuing days and in the coming years of silence, Guillaume Couture was not dead. In fact, the next three years in the life of Guillaume Couture would help to open a new window on America – a new philosophy for dealing with the original inhabitants of America. But first, he would have to survive a long, harrowing, near-fatal ordeal.

(2), (3) From: Reuben Gold Thwaites (ed.), *The Jesuit Relations and Allied Documents: Travels and Explorations of the Jesuit Missionaries in New France 1610-1791,* Burrows Brothers Company, Publishers (Cleveland OH: 1898); see ***Bibliography***

CHAPTER 5

Two weeks of torture

Running the gauntlet

The war party of two hundred that they had encountered en route continued the regime of torture, abuse and deprivation that would darken many weeks ahead. In his chilling account in the *Jesuit Relations*, Isaac Jogues recalls this day:

> "...Then we encountered a party of 200 Iroquois braves returning from a hunt. They were gleeful on seeing us, they formed two facing lines of 100 on a side, armed themselves with sticks of thorns and made us pass all naked between them down a road of fury and anguish where they let go upon us with numerous strong blows." [4]

Having suffered torture wounds following the ambush and in nightly ordeals of ceremonial abuse along the way, Guillaume and the rest of the captives were enduring agonizing discomfort in the trek through the wilderness, as the *Relations* recount, they:

> "...suffered almost insupportable torment: hunger, stifling heat, the pain of our wounds, which for not being dressed, became putrid even to breeding worms." [5]

Over the next two weeks, the captives and their captors tramped and paddled through the insect-plagued wilderness, initially along the shore of the St. Lawrence river. South of the island on which Montréal would rise, the party beached their canoes and followed a forest path to the west bank of a river recently named after New France's patron, Cardinal Richelieu, formerly and more accurately known as the River of the Iroquois. Paddling against the current in that wide valley, they journeyed south to the source of the river, a long lake stretching south, named after the founder of Québec.

From Lake Champlain, they crossed over to Lake George, having traversed the present-day State of Vermont from north to south, until they could cross into the Hudson River valley and ultimately reach the mouth of the river of the Mohawks. From there, they proceeded into the heart of Iroquois country, to the three largest 'cantons' of the main clans of the Mohawks, the most easterly nation of the Five Nations of the Iroquois Confederacy.

Situated in those days on the south side of the beautiful Mohawk river valley, generally within present-day Montgomery County, NY, these main Mohawk towns were often described at the time as "castles" by Europeans: Ossernenon, just west of the little Schoharie river (near present-day Auriesville, NY) and later the birthplace of recently canonized Saint Kateri Tekakwitha; Andagaron, about ten miles (sixteen kilometres) farther west; and, ultimately, the Mohawk 'capital' Tionnontoguen (now the hamlet of Sprakers, in the town of Root, NY).

Ossernennon was the base of the powerful Turtle Clan, whose descendants ultimately relocated to Caughnawaga outside Montréal, after having supported the losing side in the American War of Independence. Andagaron, also a base of one of the clans, would ultimately be remembered for the last days of a Christian martyr. Finally, Tionnontoguen was the main town or "castle" of the Mohawks: here the Five Nations' councils met to decide issues affecting not only the Mohawks, but the whole Iroquois Confederacy, whose expanding range and influence now stretched from west of Niagara to the Hudson River and north to the south shores of the St. Lawrence and Ottawa rivers. (Despite their prominence at the time, these towns are now lost to history, having been abandoned and their populations relocated after the devastating smallpox epidemics and subsequent French raids of the 1660s).

Throughout their tortuous – and torturous – trek, the Jesuit *Relations* report that both the Native and French captives' had their fingers broken or even lopped-off and their flesh seared with red-hot coals. For the killing of a chieftain, Guillaume endured an especially vicious regime of torture, which ironically may have saved his life.

After arriving at one Mohawk village and being subjected to repeated indignities, the *Relations* record that:

> "…*one of these barbarians, having noted that Guillaume Couture, whose hands were torn apart, had not yet lost any of his fingers, seized one of his hands and tried to cut off an index finger with a dull knife, and as he could not succeed therein, he twisted it and in tearing at it, he pulled sinew out of the arm, to the length of a span.*"[6]

Ironically, Guillaume's quiet endurance seems to have impressed his captors, who greatly respected stoic suffering. After he passed into unconsciousness, one of the clan leaders, possibly from the Onondaga Nation, suggested that Guillaume should be removed to his lodge. As a result, Guillaume was saved from the further abuses that were meted-out to the others.

[4], [5], [6] From: Reuben Gold Thwaites (ed.), *The Jesuit Relations and Allied Documents: Travels and Explorations of the Jesuit Missionaries in New France 1610-1791*, Burrows Brothers Company, Publishers (Cleveland OH: 1898); see ***Bibliography***

CHAPTER 6

Up from slavery

September, 1642 to July 5, 1645

When their health had recovered sufficiently to allow them to travel, Guillaume and Father Jogues were brought to the Mohawks' main town, Tionnontoguen. In a scene that must have reminded Guillaume of the stories of the burning of St. Joan a short distance from his house in Rouen, he witnessed the excruciating death-by-fire that ended Ahatsistari's life. An amazed Guillaume recounted to Father Jogues that his Christian convert Ahatsistari had foregone swearing the traditional death curse of Huron warriors. Remarkably, he had called-out to his Huron brethren from his execution pyre that they should end the mutually destructive cycle of attack and retribution – to find a way to make peace with the Iroquois.

The grand peace gesture of Ahatsistari had no immediate effect on the hearts of the Mohawks. Still fresh in their minds was his leadership role breaching their peace treaty with the Hurons and humiliating them in battle in 1641, despite being outnumbered four-to-one. The remaining captives, including Guillaume, René Goupil and Isaac Jogues, endured another round of physical abuse. At the end of the summer, however, tribal Elders had evidently decided that only three of the Hurons, including Ahatsistari, but none of the French should be killed. Abruptly, the tone changed.

Perhaps it was a disagreement within the Iroquois Haudenosaunee councils, or among the Iroquois clans, about the disposition of the French. Perhaps it was a reflection of a growing and begrudging admiration for

Guillaume's courage and stoicism. But whatever the cause, for Guillaume Couture, Father Isaac Jogues and René Goupil, the torture dissipated and mere slavery replaced it.

The murder of René Goupil

René Goupil had survived several months in captivity, enduring routine torture and abuse. But newly arrived in the New World, and without Couture's experience in dealing with Native culture, Goupil was vulnerable to innocent transgressions, with severe consequences. In a tragic misunderstanding, Goupil was caught administering a blessing to a child who was suffering from fever. A shaman determined that the blessing was a curse and responsible for the illness befalling the child.

Since the tribal Elders disagreed on whether the French should be killed or ransomed, the holy man evidently surreptitiously sought-out the help of a young relative to murder the physician, whom he likely saw as a purveyor of a competitive religion and diminishing the shaman's traditional authority within the tribe. As seen in other breaches of the peace, the strong cultural need for young warriors to prove themselves courageous and war-like, both to their young peers and to potential spouses, often overwhelmed their obedience to decisions by the Council, especially if urged-on by a shaman. As a result, on September 29, 1642 in the Mohawk village of Ossernenon (now Auriesville, NY), a young Mohawk brave tomahawked Goupil to death, while a shocked and helpless Guillaume was restrained nearby. Goupil was canonized as a Christian martyr and saint in 1930. For Guillaume, life in enslaved captivity continued.

Father Jogues found it equally difficult to accommodate himself to his new circumstances, but between chores and as his language facility grew, he found solace in being able to preach to a curious group of captors.

A warrior's daughter

Guillaume seemed to find comfort in the work routine, bolstered by his superior and expanding knowledge of the complex grammar of the Iroquois dialects around him. He also benefitted from a somewhat curious but understandable set of customs of the Iroquois peoples, rooted in the Great Law of the Iroquois. Clan-based and with small nuclear families, intermarriage of relatives was a concern and a taboo. As a result, the Iroquois had traditionally looked favourably on bringing new members into the tribe, typically from conquered people or captives, whether men, women or children. In fact, in later decades, the Iroquois Confederacy expanded exponentially in numbers and geographically, through the conquest of an ever-wider circle of neighbouring tribes. Following their victories, the Iroquois would kidnap survivors, or even incorporate whole vanquished tribes into the Five Nations.

One surprising early illustration of this practice was "Thérèse" Oionhaton, Guillaume's fourteen-year-old companion on the ill-fated canoe-flotilla in 1642. After her capture and subsequent disappearance, Father Jogues encountered her as part of a Mohawk fishing party, on his return to Iroquois country in May 1646. Later, in 1654, she was discovered by Father Simon Le Moyne, living with her captured sister and her own family, in a cabin in an Iroquois village in Onondaga country. The French made determined efforts to ransom her during the decade, but without success. On one occasion, she travelled three leagues over difficult terrain to rendezvous with the "Black Robes", but for some reason, the meeting failed to take place.

This unusual practice of 'inviting' the defeated enemy into your tribe and clan had a peculiar manifestation in Guillaume's case. The harsh life of an Iroquois woman depended on her ability to coax corn and sunflowers from the soil, but in particular, on the success of her husband or father in the hunt. To lose a breadwinner to war or disease was devastating for the family. To compensate, captured warriors might be assigned to an Iroquois family, initially as a slave, but if things went well, perhaps to become part of the family.

In addition to a possible romantic connection with his erstwhile "captor", another matter of the heart is hinted. If Guillaume was indeed assigned to live with the Onondagas, it is conceivable that he lived in the same settlement as Thérèse Oionhaton, with whom he had already shared so much hardship and endured much cruelty. Nothing is recorded, but one might speculate about the possibility that some form of a relationship may have developed between them: two captive youngsters in an alien land.

Her recurrent efforts to return to New France after his departure and his request to be released from his vow of celibacy before his mission to the Iroquois in 1645 suggest intriguing possibilities. By 1654, however, both were married and settled, so any youthful romance was likely a casualty to the hard life choices on the frontier and the passage of time.

Life in the Longhouse

Without practical means of escape, the remaining two Frenchmen were simply billeted among the clan longhouses. Like giant quonset huts of bark and bowed tree limbs, bunk-bed style sleeping quarters raked three levels high were provided along the length of the longhouse. In the centre, a constantly burning fire brought weak light and smoky heat to the building. It was a lifestyle that was intensely communal and designed to reinforce clan, family and collective values, over those of the individual.

Europeans brought the wider world's diseases to America for the first time. Ironically, and most insidiously the contagions were often spread between the children of settlers and those of Aboriginals, all of whom faced the perils of high rates of infant and child mortality, or with equal irony, by those selflessly ministering to the sick. The longhouse proved especially vulnerable to close-contact diseases like smallpox and measles, which wiped-out entire families with microbes that circulated in the swirling smoke of the nightly fire.

In this communal environment, all aspects of human life played-out, often in full display of extended family: restive children and sobbing infants; the arguing and love-making of adults; and, throughout, gossiping and planning, stirring and moaning, coughing and lingering illness. In these close quarters, there were few secrets.

While other captives feared for their future, Guillaume's "make the best of it" approach allowed him to settle into his new surroundings as a welcome relief from his tortured existence of August and September. Over time, with his growing proficiency in Iroquoian language, he began to answer the questions of curious Mohawks in nearby bunks, and he could query them about the customs, practices and personalities that he encountered in his daily chores. He was one of the first Europeans to understand the extensive, rich and complex oral constitution of the

Iroquois, known as the Great Law. Over time, to his captors he began to appear to be less threatening and mysterious.

To the Iroquois who came to know him, Guillaume was unlike the inflexible and culturally alien Dutch, English and French they had encountered until now, who expected the Iroquois to bend to their ways and to foreswear their beliefs. Increasingly, they came to see Guillaume as someone with practical insights on issues that mattered to the Iroquois. For his part, Guillaume began to frame his advice in the context of the subtle and balanced logic of the Great Law, and with an eye to the broader implications that his advice might have. After months of campfire storytelling and late-night conversations in the smoky darkness of the longhouse, they respected him as a trusted interpreter of a wider world that was increasingly challenging and disrupting the centuries-old Iroquois way of life. Now a familiar daily face and fluent in their dialect, while evidently understanding and respecting their complex order of speaking precedence, he seemed to be almost one of their own.

For his part, Guillaume had to overcome a number of his own cultural prejudices, some of which challenged his very conventional sense of Christian morality. In the Iroquoian societies, both Iroquois and Huron, young women were expected to marry early and have children. But they were given the latitude to select a husband of their choosing, or at least to make clear their interest in a particular member of the community. In practice, that meant a number of 'exploratory' courtships, in a fashion that shocked the traditional moral sensibilities of Father Jogues and his missionary contemporaries. A single man in his twenties, Guillaume found himself facing a challenge to another of his donné vows: chastity.

The American and Canadian frontiers were, however, also a world of 'country wives', in the quaint phrasing of the Scots of the Hudson's Bay Company. Native / French liaisons were a well established and tolerated practice by both sides, and their offspring often played a part in subsequent history, ranging from western America exploration to Louis Riel's two Métis Rebellions (in Manitoba and Saskatchewan).

As Guillaume's favourable status rose in the community, the young women of the band found him increasingly worthy of interest and a communally acceptable object of that interest, having earned the respect of the very influential women elders – the Clan mothers – in this socially matriarchal society. In the time-honoured ways of the Iroquois and the Huron, they let him know their interest in the most unmistakable and occasionally demonstrable fashion. Understandably, the priests' otherwise meticulous history of those years does not record such incidents. But we can speculate, in part based on subsequent events.

Adoption by a warrior's widow

Guillaume's situation was particularly remarkable. Having killed a prominent young Iroquois leader and being evidently more fit and able than his French compatriots, Guillaume was apparently awarded to an unnamed Onondaga war widow, as compensation. While one might imagine the circumstances to be untenable – living with a killer – the hard realities of wilderness life called for a more practical assessment by the woman involved. To enhance his acceptability, the Elders observed that he was apparently fearless, both in battle and under torture. Unlike most Europeans they had encountered, Guillaume knew the forests well and he was a good hunter and fisherman. She knew painfully of his demonstrated skill with his own firearm and yet, he seemed a pleasant young man and he had mastered the local dialect better than most captives. On balance, he would be a valuable member of the hunt and he would keep their winter larder full.

For his part, Guillaume settled into life among the Iroquois with declining resentment and increasing interest. His flexible, broad-minded approach to life served him well. An open and pliant perspective seemed to keep him from committing the kinds of faux pas to which his French colleagues too often fell victim. Frenchmen, he knew, could be innocent or insensitive to their circumstances, whether pursuing religious ardour or evincing a shocked reaction to Native practices that offended their European values. He was determined to avoid the same fate as his beloved friend René.

Ihandich

Unable to use his wounded hands in his carpentry trade, Guillaume busied himself with other manual, domestic chores, like repairing dwellings and sewing hides. The Iroquois gently mocked his willingness to do this 'woman's work', including the challenge of using his damaged fingers to sew with quills. Whether it was 'Guillaume' or 'Cousture', the Jesuit history recorded that the Natives found the sound of his French name distasteful for some reason, so a nickname was in order. Borrowing from the Hurons, the Iroquois awarded Couture the mildly derisive nickname "Ihandich", 'the one who sews'.

Guillaume's keen powers of observation and imitation had served him well in learning the Iroquoian languages and cultures of the Huron, the Mohawk and the Onondaga, as they had earlier, with the Algonquin-based languages and folkways of the Ottawa and the Montagnais. Unlike many Europeans of his day, his capacity to communicate in Native tongues accelerated his ability to absorb forest lore and cultural norms, both of which helped to keep him in good graces with his often-unpredictable captors. It proved especially valuable in appreciating the subtle nuances of Iroquoian language and more crucially, their social, political and philosophical norms. His capacity involved a sophisticated understanding beyond most Europeans, who communicated with a limited mixture of hand-signals, pidgin language and suspect third-party interpreters. Often with disastrous consequences, these shortcomings too often made Iroquois motivations, objectives, tensions and concerns impenetrable to Europeans.

As time wore on, Guillaume took this ability one step further. Not knowing how an enemy slave should act to keep safe, and trying to earn the latitude needed to plan an escape, he found himself increasingly "filling the moccasins" of the warrior he had 'replaced'. He tried to act as his Native counterpart would have acted, on the hunt, in the fields and forests, in his dress and in his conversation. As the months of winter and spring rolled-by, he became a comfortable companion of the band of young men sustaining the village and the clan.

Over time, around fishing-party campfires and during long dark nights in the crowded smoky longhouse, Guillaume was invited to answer questions from Iroquois who were curious about the unknown wider world that he represented. Topics ranged from religion, family life and strange European customs, to elemental explanations of craftsmanship, physics and astronomy. Respected tribal Elders also noted his practical advice and distinctive observations. Couture began to be invited to attend and observe the general councils where much of the clan and tribal business was debated and decided. Among the Iroquois, he noted, an ability to speak persuasively and with authority counted for a great deal.

Ransoming the captives

Unknown to Guillaume and Father Jogues, some of the Iroquois leaders were curious about the value of their hostages and the commercial trade leverage that they might afford. They let it be known to nearby Europeans in New Netherlands that the Frenchmen might not be dead after all, neglecting to mention the fate of Goupil and the other unnamed Frenchman. Over the winter, this news was communicated back through the Dutch at Fort Orange (Albany NY) and New Amsterdam (Manhattan) to their royal patrons, and through them to their French 'cousins', that the Jesuit Father Jogues might still be alive.

In Paris, Louis XIII's wife, Queen Anne of Austria, intervened personally with a ransom offer of 260 piastres (roughly 260 silver 'pieces of eight'). Subsequent negotiations between New Netherlands officials and the Mohawks failed, ironically because the Governor of New Netherlands came in person, at the French Queen's behest. The status-conscious Iroquois concluded that such a prominent emissary meant that the captives might be more valuable than they had originally imagined. This change in view by the Iroquois may have helped to improve respect and living conditions for Father Jogues and Guillaume, but it also caused the Iroquois to reconsider their geo-political strategy with the French. As always, the Mohawks and the Onondagas, in particular, were canny and strategic negotiators.

All of these developments were unknown to the captives. The two Frenchmen continued on their daily course of domestic chores and occasional foraging for game, fish and furs. In November 1643, Couture and Jogues were taken as bearers on a late fall fishing trip along the not-yet-frozen Mohawk River. Over the evening's campfire, the two Frenchmen quietly reflected on the fact that it was the anniversary of Goupil's murder. This latest sojourn brought them very close to the increasingly numerous Dutch traders along the Mohawk and the Hudson river valleys, centering on Fort Orange. The Iroquois evidently hoped that they might supplement their catch with some trade goods, if they encountered a Dutch vessel.

While the captives were unaware of the efforts to secure their release, local Dutch merchants likely knew of both the failed negotiations and the rejected ransom offer. When the Iroquois spotted a little trading sloop on the river near their encampment, they signaled their wish to trade – and Guillaume saw his opportunity. As in the 1642 ambush, however, his first thought was his duty to his vow of service and to Father Jogues. He decided that he would smuggle the priest onto the boat when it anchored in the reeds, while the Mohawks were busy haggling for trade goods. His own opportunity would have to come later.

It was a risky move, as he knew the Dutch had little use for the Catholic French, especially Jesuits, after decades of Dutch independence wars and Spanish Catholic oppression. They might simply turn him back to the Mohawks, to curry favour with the Iroquois. A successful escape was also likely to attract a vigourous reaction from his captors, who would recognize Guillaume's role in facilitating the priest's escape. Once again, Couture chose courage over caution, and hid the priest in a location where he could board the vessel undetected by the Natives.

As it turned out, Guillaume's gamble was successful. The Dutch decided that it was worth the risk to free their fellow European, probably aided by knowledge of a recent alliance of convenience against Spain between the Netherlands Republic and the King of France. When the boat weighed anchor and the Mohawks realized the escape, they decided that the priest had made good his own escape and evidently were impressed that Couture did not take the opportunity to do the same.

As a result, Guillaume was doomed to at least a further winter of enslavement. But his stature was steadily rising among his captors, bolstered by particularly by his decision to stay with them, when his countryman fled. He was also being seen as less of a boy and more as a man.

The 'ghost' of Isaac Jogues

Meanwhile, Father Jogues navigated a perilous and circuitous route back to France, from Manhattan by way of England, eventually returning to the Jesuit motherhouse in Paris. By now presumed dead and seen as a martyr, his ghostly reappearance was a cause of great joy and celebration among the clergy, who had been praying for his departed soul.

While in France, Father Jogues completed the written record of his amazing exploits in the New World, most notably his capture and captivity among the much-feared Iroquois, who were attacking New France with great success. Among the tales of death and misery in the mission fields of America, however, one of the most prominent characters in his story was not a priest or a Native chief, but a simple lay missionary – a donné. The courage, piety and selfless devotion of this donné were chronicled by Jogues – and Jogues could write with unmatched authority on such things. Knowing that he would likely be dead by now, Jogues felt that his name and his contributions to New France and Christianity should be recorded for posterity: 'le bon Cousture'.

Within the year, rested and healing from his mutilations, and despite believing that he had lost all of his colleagues from his last mission tour, Jogues was seeking permission to return to New France and to his Huron missions.

A man of the tribe

Back in Iroquois country, Couture continued with daily life among his captors.

After years in Iroquois country, his European clothing had long since disappeared into rags. From both necessity and affectation, he had adopted Iroquois dress. Lately, he was persuaded to adopt manly Iroquois appearance, which often involved painting the face in cobalt blue and deep clay yellow, as well as cutting one's hair in the distinctive Mohawk fashion. Thus attired, he drew less and less attention as he took a place at the edge of the long-house debates, and more recently, answering questions on the topics under discussion and even tentatively volunteering his opinions, or whispering suggestions to more appropriate spokesmen.

Now more regularly engaged to help the councils of the Iroquois understand the intentions of the Europeans, the maturing Couture's status continued to grow. Almost imperceptibly, he evolved from the status of slave and captive, to formal 'hostage', and ultimately, to informal counselor. More and more, he assumed in their eyes and his own, the persona and role of the dead Iroquois captain whom he had 'replaced'.

Couture paid increasing attention to the intentions, tensions and motivations influencing their leaders. His growing mastery of the Iroquois language and its dialects allowed him to appreciate the subtle nuances and varying viewpoints reflected in the councils of the Haudenosaunee. It would soon make him invaluable in navigating the rhetoric and distrust besetting the diplomacy between the Iroquois and the French (and their Native allies).

As one of the subsequent *Jesuit Relations* reported:

> "...the Iroquois held him in esteem and high repute, as one of the first men in their nation. Consequently he assumed the position of a captain among them, having acquired this prestige by his prudence and wisdom." [7]

In fact, history records that no other 'foreigner', neither Native nor European, neither before nor afterwards, ever again achieved the status of a full member of the council.

As mentioned earlier, the name(s) "Guillaume" or "Couture" appeared to have an unpleasant sound or connotation in the Mohawk dialect, so he quickly acquired a nickname, "Ihandich". Reflecting on his initial courage and subsequent exploits in the hunt, however, his captors gradually found that gently derisive and effeminate moniker inappropriate. Initially with mocking humour, but later with increasingly admiration, they came to address Couture as "Achirra", which variously translates as 'the worthy' or even 'superman'. Clearly, after several years, Couture was no longer seen as a captive foreigner or an enemy slave, but more and more as an adopted and near-equal member of the Iroquois family.

---

[7] From: Reuben Gold Thwaites (ed.), *The Jesuit Relations and Allied Documents: Travels and Explorations of the Jesuit Missionaries in New France 1610-1791*, Burrows Brothers Company, Publishers (Cleveland OH: 1898); see **Bibliography**

CHAPTER 7

A 'ghost' bringing peace

An offer of peace

When their captives were not within earshot, many Elders in the Iroquois villages again began to think it might be wiser to ransom the French than to kill them. There was even discussion of whether they might be used as a good-will gesture, to open diplomatic channels with the French. The Iroquois had allied themselves with the Dutch, and on occasion, with the English, to harry the French. But Iroquois tradition argued for independence of action and preeminence in alliances. Playing the Europeans against one another might be a shrewder course.

In fact, many Mohawks were becoming concerned about their Dutch and English neighbours, who were arriving in increasing numbers. Moreover, unlike the French, the English cleared the land and laid-out road networks. They were pushing westward into the lands of the Iroquois, and would be hard to resist. For their part, the French and their Huron allies had proved formidable in past wars. With their focus on furs, waterways and trading posts, rather than farming, towns and road-building, the French seemed inherently more sympathetic and reconcilable to Native interests than the encroaching British and Dutch settlers along their Hudson valley frontier.

While this debate continued among the Iroquois, fate intervened. In early 1645, Champlain's successor as Governor of New France, Charles Huault de Montmagny, extended an olive branch: an offer to 'parlay' at Trois-Rivières. The Iroquois knew Montmagny as a determined adversary for nearly a decade, translating his name 'mont magny' as 'great mountain', or "Orontio", a name that both Hurons and Iroquois came to use for all French Governors over time.

Should they go? The Iroquois shamans and chieftains and Clan Mothers were not able to agree among themselves whether going to Trois-Rivières was a good idea.

As Couture had come to realize, within the Haudenosaunee, decisions of the majority of leaders did not necessarily bind all. Those who were unhappy with the decision could act alone, especially if they had clan support, as the shaman had done with Goupil's murder, with little fear of sanction beyond reproach. It was a confusing and complex society within which Couture was becoming imbued – and one replete with the risks of opting-out and even betrayal.

From Benjamin Franklin and other drafters of the American Constitution, there are accounts of the *Gayanashagowa* or the *Great Law of Peace* of the Iroquois Confederacy. It was a complex, consensus-based, almost federal decision-making structure, replete with its skein of checks-and-balances on the nations and clans of the Iroquois Haudenosaunee. In this pre-literate society, the provisions and meanings of each of the 117 sections of this elaborate 'oral constitution' were recalled by the symbols, as 'memory prompts', embedded in beaded wampum belts passed down from Deganwidah, the Great Peacemaker, and his spokesman, Hiawatha.

After several years in captivity, Couture had likely heard the rote recitation of the Great Law by shamans at many a fireside and individual sections cited by Haudenosaunee orators. The resulting subtle and intricate decision-making system manifested itself with increasing clarity to Couture, as he sat listening to their debates. To someone familiar with the colonial manifestations of a decision-making system descending from the absolute monarchy of the French kings and the authority of feudal nobility, it was an education. The Great Law sometimes seemed like a system designed to restrain collective action and to prohibit majority rule – with patient consensus, erudite persuasion and non-committal acquiescence appearing to be the basis for major decisions. (Perhaps that is the basis of its subsequent historical appeal to American constitutional culture?)

In the absence of majority rule or kingship to impose decisions, the key consideration in securing support or acquiescence in Iroquois circles was often the rhetorical persuasiveness of the proponent – or opponent – in council. As was recorded afterwards, among the Mohawks in particular, eloquence ranked only behind bravery in the hunt and in war for status in their community. In fact, especially gifted orators might be engaged to speak on behalf of tribal leaders, rather than on their own behalf, to help carry the day on an important issue.

The case for peace

Couture observed that one orator in particular, whose main physical feature was his long hooked nose, could speak with a skill and persuasiveness that few could match. That raised an interesting prospect. If that leader could be convinced to adopt a favourable policy toward the French, he had the influence to persuade many others. An entente between the French and the Iroquois might end the half-century of warfare that kept the French huddled on the north shore of the St. Lawrence, and many more French unwilling to leave Europe for America.

If peace could be secured – and given the strategic location of the broad and expanding sphere of influence of the Iroquois – there was the very real prospect of opening the heart of America to the French, through the Great Lakes and beyond the Appalachians. With that alliance, across a network of great lakes and rivers that would soon be 'discovered' and named by French explorers, leading to the Missouri and Mississippi, French trade and evangelism could be spread among the Nations of the continent's interior.

Couture had lived among the Montagnais and the Huron and he had come to know the Algonquin. From his years with them, and despite his lack of formal education, he could see that the robust and prosperous Iroquois Confederacy was ascendant and that Champlain's decision to ally himself with the bellicose Hurons against the powerful and sophisticated Iroquois confederation of nations was likely a mistake of major historic and strategic proportions. From the Jesuits, he had learned that they, too, now quietly shared that conclusion. However, after long association with the enemies of the Iroquois, and many years of relentless Iroquois assaults on French outposts, it was an unpopular viewpoint and one that Guillaume kept to himself, for now.

The economy of North America was changing. Farming and logging were taking hold. The fur trade was being propelled farther inland, with development and over-trapping depleting the resource, as it had already done in Iroquois, Huron and Algonquin country. A peace treaty with the Iroquois, or even just their main nations, like the Mohawks and the Onondagas, might advance the interests of both the French and Iroquois. It might also secure some measure of protection for the Hurons and the Algonquins, who otherwise faced a likely future of unequal warfare and imminent economic collapse.

Having risked his life and seen his friends die for their faith, he felt strongly that the French owed a debt of religious loyalty to the Christians among the Natives, who might otherwise be exterminated in the on-going campaigns of the well-armed Iroquois. The more he thought about it, the more determined Couture became to make the case to the leaders of the Iroquois, and in particular, to the erudite Kiotseaeton, whom the French later called "Le Crochet", the Hook. Through the spring of 1645, Couture found opportunities to advance this idea with Kiotseaeton.

In late spring, the Council met to discuss its response to the French. Kiotseaeton argued for a change in policy – to accept the French offer of a parlay leading to a comprehensive peace. He spoke eloquently, inviting Couture to confirm his assertion that the French were well intentioned and that they would treat the Iroquois as equals and partners.

Clad in deerskins and moccasins, with his scalp shaved but for the iconic Mohawk arc of short-cropped hair, Couture stood at the edge of the Council fire as the epic debate ebbed and flowed. Before dawn, the Council decided that the French offer was worth pursuing, not only on behalf of the Mohawks but all of the Iroquois nations. At the peak of his influence and persuasive powers, Kiotseaeton made one other surprising proposal, to which the Council readily consented. Completing a stunning transformation three years in the making, Couture would form part of the Iroquois delegation to meet with the French, with a mandate to persuade the French to the merit and sincerity of Iroquois plans for a comprehensive peace and commercial relationship.

Couture returns to New France

In late June, the Iroquois party set-out from Tionnontoguen, with Kiotseaeton in the lead canoe and with Couture paddling with a team of his Mohawk colleagues, ironically retracing the harrowing trek of August 1642. Descending the Richelieu River, the flotilla turned into the current of the broad St. Lawrence, crossing to the north shore. The advance party arrived in Trois-Rivières on July 5, 1645 and promptly proposed to the local garrison that the French and Iroquois begin their negotiations the following week. The French immediately dispatched a courier to tell "Orontio" in Québec.

To encourage the Iroquois to consider the French peace overture, Governor Huault de Montmagny had proposed that the parlay take place in the village of Trois-Rivières, at the far western frontier of New France, immediately adjacent to the traditional range of the Iroquois. The plan must have sounded audacious to the local commander of Trois-Rivières, François de Champflour – to welcome within the walls of their tiny, palisaded compound the very warriors who had brought so much death and loss to inhabitants of Trois-Rivières during its brief existence.

When Huault de Montmagny left Québec, his entourage also included a surprising participant. After his circuitous journey, from New Amsterdam to England, and ultimately to Paris, Father Jogues received consent from the Jesuits to return to the New France missions. Newly arrived from France, Father Jogues was asked by the Governor to join him, since he had more experience with the Iroquois than most, albeit not a favourable experience. Ironically, Isaac Jogues and the rest of the French believed Couture to have been killed by those now seeking to make peace.

The Iroquois party presented themselves in Trois-Rivières on July 12th, including Couture in full Iroquois dress. As the groups assembled and faced one another, Couture spoke-up and was surprised to receive no immediate response. Of course, the French were convinced he was dead or in slavery, so hearing a man dressed as an Iroquois speak to them in French about Guillaume Couture was confusing. As the realization dawned, however, a ripple of recognition and joy spread through the ranks of the French. For their part, the Iroquois were delighted that their gambit seemed to be working and that he was evidently a person of great value and importance among the French. In the 1645 *Jesuit Relations*, the incident is recorded this way…

> *"As soon as Couture was recognized, each person threw himself on his neck. They looked on him as a man come back to life who gives joy to all who thought him dead, or at least in danger of spending the rest of his existence in a most bitter and barbarous captivity."* [8]

As the negotiations progressed, Couture found himself advancing the notion of a comprehensive peace among all the Aboriginal nations – Iroquois, Huron and Algonquin – and not just between the Iroquois and the French. This concept went well beyond what either most of the French or most of the Iroquois had in mind. After a half-century of continuous warfare, the entente was to be more akin to an armistice than a heart-felt peace treaty. Eager to secure a respite from unrelenting attacks, the French authorities were conducting behind the scenes discussions unknown to Couture, which threatened to leave the Iroquois a free hand to deal with their long-standing enemies, the Huron and the Algonquin, as long as an effort was made to avoid attacking those who had accepted Christianity.

Couture seems to have envisaged an historic new social and economic relationship in which the French moved freely among the Native tribes in a network supporting the French fur trade and missionary work, while leaving the interior unsettled by the French, except for the occasional fortified trading post. This concept, which has echoes in the vision of Tecumseh and the Prophet at the beginning of the 19th century, found considerable appeal among the Iroquois, as it broke the decades-old Huron and Algonquin fur-trade monopoly with the French. More strategically, it gave the Iroquois a new market for their furs and source of European goods, while giving them new leverage with the Europeans to the south. By now, they were eager to avoid more of the pattern of settlement that was encroaching on their lands from New Netherlands in the south and, in particular, from New England in the east.

Although it failed to take immediate root at Trois-Rivières in the summer of 1645, the seeds of a comprehensive and pragmatic relationship were sewn by "Ihandich" (he who sews, as Couture was now known to them). With interruptions, it proved to be the pattern of French involvement across North America for the next hundred years, and beyond. But for it to become established between two such bitter and suspicious enemies – the French and the Iroquois – someone would have to persuade all the clans and all the nations of the Iroquois, and those beyond. Of equal challenge, someone who knew the Hurons and the Iroquois equally well was needed to mediate the peace prayed for by Ahatsistari on his funeral pyre. The leaders of the Iroquois and the French concluded and agreed that only one man could be trusted to advance Couture's ambitious vision – Couture himself.

An ambassador of peace

As a result, Couture undertook the role of peace ambassador, travelling throughout the Iroquois and Huron country during the summer of 1645 and the winter of 1646. The discussions proceeded very well among the war-weary Native communities, although old enmities remained fresh and just below the surface. The loss of commercial advantage represented a major loss to the power and prestige of the Hurons and the Algonquins. The Iroquois shamans continued to be threatened by the Black Robes and their religion, blaming them for recurrent illness and crop failures that were the vengeance of the 'old gods'. The negotiations were difficult and the risk of isolated provocations undoing tentative agreements was ever-present.

In the spring of 1646, Couture returned to Québec to report significant progress in the negotiations, with a comprehensive peace in reach. The 'bridge building' he was doing between the Native communities and the French took a surprising turn on his return to New France. His role as a humble donné was only a vague memory by now. Still, as ambassador plenipotentiary for the Colony, he was nonetheless very conscious of his continuing religious vows of poverty, obedience and chastity, sworn at the behest of the Jesuits many years ago. Perhaps anticipating an opportunity to cement relations through marriage, at the ripe age of 29, the ever-dutiful Couture formally requested release from his vow of chastity, leaving him in the eyes of the church, free to marry. The consent was granted by a worldly future saint and martyr, the Jesuit Superior in Québec, Father Gabriel Lalemant, on April 26, 1646.

Couture moved the complex negotiations forward aggressively throughout 1646, inviting a succession of delegations from the various Native nations to meet with him and French colonial officials at Trois-Rivières and at Québec. However, just as a breakthrough seemed imminent, or perhaps because of that, murders in Huron country by some disaffected Iroquois brought discussions to an abrupt halt and raised the prospect of renewed hostilities.

While formerly a missionary to the Hurons, Father Jogues had used his time as an Iroquois captive to establish the foundation for mission work among the Mohawks. He made three modestly successful voyages in Iroquois county, and was undertaking his forth with his companion Jean De La Lande, when both were murdered on October 18th, 1646. As soon as word of this treachery reached the French, negotiations were abruptly terminated. For their part, despite their grievous losses to war and disease, the Hurons and the Algonquins were quietly pleased with the failure of the negotiations. Local self-interest and distrust of the Iroquois prevailed over Couture's loftier goals.

Undaunted, Couture undertook a new tact, by initiating an embassy to the increasingly beleaguered Hurons in the winter of 1646-47. He sat by their campfires as they celebrated their new feast – Christmas – singing the Huron Carol that Father Brébeuf had composed for them in their language, some time around 1643. [9]

Around the Council fires, Couture made the case for peace, but war was the order of the day, with constant attacks from the ascendant Iroquois. By now, both sides seemed too locked in the death-struggle to consider compromise.

The Hurons and the Algonquins clung to their privileged trade-intermediary position, despite the declining fur resources within their own territories and the new routes to European markets that were being forged by both Native tribes and Europeans. The Iroquois seemed to believe that they could establish their dominant position in relation to the French by subjugating or exterminating the Huron and marginalizing the Algonquins, a strategy that ultimately worked.

In the spring of 1649, the position of both the Hurons and the French in Huronia had become untenable. Ste-Marie-among-the-Hurons, which Couture and others had constructed, was evacuated and burned by the

French and Christian Hurons. The moment for the dream articulated by Couture and Kiotseaeton had passed and its revival would need to await new actors and new economic and political realities.

Return of Achirra – the 'worthy Couture'

Despite his 'failures', Couture's personal standing among all Indian nations was at its zenith. His efforts and his safe return to New France was welcomed with great relief by French and Aboriginal alike. Father Jacques Buteux, the long-time pastor of the congregation at the outpost of Trois-Rivières, and who would immortalize him in a 1652 Jesuit report with the title "the worthy Couture", led his Christian Aboriginal converts in a grand "welcome home" celebration at Trois-Rivières in 1647. Later, as Couture progressed eastward, the celebration of his efforts was repeated in Sillery, near Québec…*"with joy on the part of all the Huron, Algonkin and Anniehronnon [Mohawk] Indians,"* the *Journal des Jésuites* later noted. [10]

When the festivities were behind him, Couture told his friends and the Jesuits that he had had enough of adventure and wanted to settle down. Who could blame him for wanting some peace and a more conventional life, like the one he left in Rouen? Still, that new life seemed unlikely to those who knew him and his history. The irony deepened when he indicated his choice for domestic repose: he would clear a farm on the deadly, foreboding south shore of the St. Lawrence opposite the heights of Québec, where no European had dared take-up residence for in the whole of the 17th century, and survived.

[8], [10] From: Reuben Gold Thwaites (ed.), *The Jesuit Relations and Allied Documents: Travels and Explorations of the Jesuit Missionaries in New France 1610-1791*, Burrows Brothers Company, Publishers (Cleveland OH: 1898); see **Bibliography**

[9] Each Holiday season, most North Americans hear the words of the popular, Middleton translation of the Huron Carol; the actual words composed in the Huron Wendat language by Father Jean-de-Brébeuf are somewhat different. See: http://www.wyandot.org/carol.htm

CHAPTER 8

Life on the deadly shore

A wilderness farm with a wonderful view

Couture's lands at present-day Lévis, Québec (the Pointe-de-Lévy or Pointe-Lévy) directly faced the ramparts of the village Québec, then a short summer canoe-paddle across the narrowing St. Lawrence and a promising location for game, fish and even farming. Yet these lands were conspicuously unoccupied, despite the growth of both French and Native settlement along the north shore and on Orléans Island.

The lands around the Pointe-de-Lévy were the traditional lands of the tribes that traversed the St. Lawrence to trade with the French, such as the Montagnais and the Algonquins, but they raised no dwellings there. These lands were handy to Québec and fertile for farming, but French settlers preferred the less promising soil on the north shore and would not build across the river. Above all, these lands were known to one and all as "Iroquois country". Others might have a legal, traditional or geographic claim, but the Iroquois exerted unchallenged and deadly control.

The Pointe-de-Lévy lands and more along the south shore were grandly designated a Seigneury by King Louis XIII – a feudal 'duchy' owned and overseen by Lord Jean de Lauson, but from the comfort and safety of his manor home in France. The Lauzon Seigneury had been created and granted on condition that it should encourage settlement by immigrants to New France. But for obviously reasons, few were interested, even with very nominal terms requiring the land to be cleared and a house to be erected. Every immigrant soon learned that a reawakening of hostilities with the Iroquois could quickly cost a settler and his family their labour, their home and likely their lives.

Into this inauspicious picture stepped Guillaume Couture. An ambitious Québec settler, François Byssot de la Rivière (also subsequently spelled "Bissot") met Couture and realized the potential to exploit this opportunity as a mutually beneficial business partnership. Couture's time with the Jesuits and the Iroquois was much admired by all, but it also had ensured his faithfulness to his vow of poverty and left him almost penniless. He had the desire to carve-out a new life for himself, but he lacked the means.

Couture was, nonetheless, an experienced carpenter and woodsman from his time in Tadoussac and Huronia. More importantly, his relations with the Iroquois improved his prospects and those under his protection, of living on the south shore unmolested, irrespective of the prevailing state of affairs between the French authorities and the various Indian nations, including especially the Iroquois. For his part, Byssot had some money and access to the kinds of provisions and materials that would be necessary to settle a virgin forest tract.

After returning from his last embassy to the Hurons in 1647, Couture entered into a partnership with Byssot. Couture agreed to clear for Byssot a long, narrow parcel of land back from the shore, and then to erect a house in which Byssot could live, on condition that Couture – his "insurance policy" – would develop and settle on the land next to him. Meanwhile, Byssot lived in Québec. When Couture completed the agreed work in late 1647, Byssot paid Couture a sum of 200 livres and let him live in the new house until Couture could repeat the process for himself, the following spring. By the middle of 1648, Couture had built a country farmhouse and cleared a parallel farm plot for himself, fronting on the St. Lawrence – the highway of the colony. Since the row-homes of the village and his home in Rouen were not suitable models, carpenter Couture built a house of his own design, with a steep-pitched roof against the accumulation of winter snow, a fieldstone fireplace for heat and cooking, and a grand porch from which to watch life of the colony play out on the river before him.

A man of property

As both Couture and Byssot had now completed the conditions necessary to qualify for a homesteader's land grant, Seigneur de Lauson granted Couture (and Byssot) title to their land, in documents dated October 15, 1648. Couture thus became the first European colonist to establish himself successfully and legally on the south shore of the St. Lawrence River. In doing so, beginning with Byssot, he initiated an ever-widening settlement of French-speaking farmers and townsfolk that continued for three centuries thereafter. But before this breakthrough was celebrated, New France held its breath. Could the treacherous south shore really be colonized, even by someone with the credentials of Guillaume Couture?

During his years in captivity, Couture imagined a peaceable life, surrounded by a wife and family, in a house built with his own hands, in this New World that offered so much freedom and potential. At times, realizing that dream must have seemed a very remote prospect. But now, it was in reach. Having installed the last shingles on the steep-pitched roof, just as the heavy late autumn snow began to fall, he lit his pipe of Indian tobacco, looked out at the sun setting on the narrowing St. Lawrence River, and reflected on his accomplishments. To Canadians, it evokes images from Gilles Vigneault's folk ballad, *"Mon Pays, C'est l'hiver"* (*"My country is winter"*), with scenes of powdery snow and ancestral home. [11]

Trusted as was he was by all sides, the colonial authorities requested Couture to be responsible for the custody of Iroquois prisoners taken in one of the recurrent outbreaks of hostilities among the French, the Iroquois and their Native adversaries. When the shaky truces periodically collapsed, such as in 1657-58, Couture found himself unmolested by Iroquois raiding parties. His immunity from harm was all the more remarkable in contrast to the dangers experienced by others.

The era saw such celebrated events as the raid on Tadoussac in 1658, at the eastern extreme of New France, far from Iroquois territory. Those attackers spent a long and worrisome night (for Couture's family), at his farm on their return trip, but left them unscathed. Other battles included the Orléans island raid on the Christian Hurons in 1656, Dollard des Ormeaux's heroic stand to save Ville-Marie (Montréal) in 1660 at

Long-Sault, the Lachine Massacre in 1689, and the legendary defense of Verchères by young Madeleine Jarret in 1692. Over the last half of the 17th century, his more positive (and secure) experience encouraged others to join Couture's little settlement on the 'dangerous' south shore.

Eligible bachelor

In a tiny community where the men were too often drawn to the wilderness and all it offered, Couture was an eligible, thirty-year-old bachelor, acclaimed by his community and its leaders. He was a mature and proven provider, with a new farm and farmhouse, and with his life of adventure allegedly behind him. For the young women of good families, and for the parents of marriageable daughters, Guillaume Couture had much to offer – and he would not remain unattached for long!

Within a year, the bans were being read for a proposed marriage between Guillaume Couture and Anne, one of the three Esmard (Aymard) sisters, who had come out together from Niort in the west-central French Province of Poitou. (Her sisters, Barbe and Madeleine, likewise married men whose family names have also come down to us as familiar surnames in Québec: Letardif and Cloutier). On November 18, 1649, in Couture's new little house at Pointe-de-Lévy, Abbé Le Sueur officiated at the first Christian marriage ceremony on the south shore of the St. Lawrence. Remarkably, the marriage license is still preserved in the records of the Church of Notre-Dame in Québec.

Anne and Guillaume settled into married life, beginning a family that would eventually grow to ten children. In 1656, as the little colony neared the half-century since Champlain had founded Québec, Couture was well along in his life as a farmer and father on the opposite shore. As the snow fell on his house on Pointe-de-Lévy that Christmas Eve, he and Anne and their neighbours sat down to a midnight meal of game-pie and Indian corn, thick soups made with their garden peas, and plates of white beans and pork flavoured with spring syrup from their maple trees. Surrounded by their children, they sang the 'response' songs that kept Couture and other inveterate canoeists rhythmically paddling through endless days on the rivers of North America for three centuries.

They also sang the Huron Carol – the hymn that Couture first heard sung in the language of the Hurons, so many years ago at Ste-Marie-among-the-Hurons. This autumn, he had had to build a bigger dining table for the season of Noël, as his family continued to expand. Arrayed around Anne were the faces of their children – Jean-Baptiste, Anne, Louis and Marguerite.

In fact, Couture was sufficiently prosperous to consider purchasing a Québec townhouse for his periodic trips to across the often ice-clogged or stormy river. Right now, all he could afford was the building lot, at 53 Rue Sous-le-Fort, in the Lower Town, so he took title to the town lot 2285. (As luck would have it, he could not find the time to pursue that venture. It was only after Couture's triumphant return to Québec in September 1666 that he and his sons could build the house. By then, life on the farm was all consuming, so he sold the completed town house the following year).

As the year 1657 dawned, it held the promise of continuing slow, steady progress for the young and growing settlement in the Seigneury of Lauzon.

But fate had a way of finding Couture – and his adventures were not yet at an end.

---

[11]   See: http://zocalopoets.com/2011/12/22/mon-pays-cest-lhiver-quebecitude-in-song/

CHAPTER 9

Ambassador and Explorer

Mission to the Onondagas:

In a small colony lodged in the immensity of North America, the few who could speak the New World's languages and who knew its ways were invaluable. Even more rare, in this land of frontiersmen and fortune-seekers, were experienced men who could be trusted simultaneously by the authorities of Church and State and the Native nations.

It was in that context that Couture was asked to leave his farm and to participate in an expedition deep into the interior of eastern North America in 1657. While he was reluctant to go, the cause was one very dear to him. He knew the Onondagas well, and they knew and respected him, having adopted him during his Iroquois captivity. Possibly the most powerful of the Iroquois nations after the Mohawks, the leaders of the Onondagas had become persuaded to the idea that better relations with the French would serve the interests of the tribe. To demonstrate their seriousness, they petitioned the Jesuits to establish a mission station in their midst, in an area that is now western New York State.

Since the demise of the Huron confederacy in 1649 and the subsequent Mohawk slaughter of the Christian Hurons' refugee encampment on nearby Orléans Island in 1656, Couture was even more convinced that peace and prosperity for the French depended on better relations with the Five Nations of the Iroquois Confederacy. From conversations with his Native contacts, he knew the Iroquois sphere of influence now extended much farther – north as far as Cree country south of Hudson Bay, on both sides of James Bay, and as far west and south as the Hudson River valley and present-day Pennsylvania, and beyond, as their war parties harried the Huron (Wyandot) refugees and their protectors as far west as Illinois, Ohio and northern Michigan.

With Couture as the subtle translator and trusted emissary between the Onondagas and the French, the Jesuits were accepted and the mission was successfully established. Couture knew from his own observation that this development would also contribute a moderating influence with the councils of the Haudenosaunee against the often bellicose, anti-French intentions of their Mohawk and Oneida compatriots. He was well pleased with this venture on his return to his farm in 1657.

In fact, while the Oneida massacre of a French party later that year brought an end to the formal 'armistice', he was more successful than he realized. As a result of his work, the Onondagas broke with the other four nations of the Iroquois and did not actively participate in the decades-long warfare that the Iroquois launched on the French after the British acquired New Netherlands (New York State) in the 1660s. The absence of the Onondagas ultimately likely made less effective the British-promoted, continuous Iroquois assault on the settlements of New France in the so-called Beaver Wars.

The Iroquois did not, however, abandon their English patrons. They used English arms and logistical support to expand the far-ranging Iroquois sphere of influence into the Ohio valley and across the western Great Lakes. A number of western tribes – including such notable Nations as the Sioux, the Shawnee, the Susquehannock, and the Miami – were defeated and driven from their traditional homes in Ohio, western Maryland, Pennsylvania, Indiana, Illinois, Michigan, Wisconsin and southern Ontario, or absorbed into the Iroquois family.

Reports of these wars and their consequences reinforced Couture's sense that the Iroquois were the most valuable group of Aboriginal allies, if not for their loyalty, then for their military power and strategic position. Later, the Iroquois began to hear from their Tuscarora kinfolk in Carolina about the waves of new English settlers and their African slaves. Soon they were to see their own newly conquered territories being encroached upon by settlers from the south in Maryland and Pennsylvania, and from the east across the Hudson River. Only then did the Iroquois begin to think seriously again about a truly collaborative peace treaty, along the lines that Couture had argued.

With their western frontier and new hunting grounds now secure but at risk from resurgent Ojibway and other tribes, the Iroquois would ultimately begin to see better relations with their traditional French and Aboriginal adversaries as potentially more promising guarantees of security and prosperity over time. But amid the flush of Iroquois victories over adversaries on all sides, and with an increasing trade dominance that they so coveted, this realization would not emerge among the Iroquois until much later in the 17th century.

In the subsequent "French and Indian Wars" of the mid-18th century, all of the Native nations faced American settler expansionism, with militias led by such notables as General George Washington. In an intriguing historical role-reversal, the British would conquer the French, but then adopt the French policy towards respecting Aboriginal rights and curbing American settlers' expansion. The French and British would try, ultimately unsuccessfully, to retain the Ohio and Mississippi valleys and the Great Lakes region for their Native allies. For their part, those periodically united Native nations faced relentless American expansionism and what today we might call the 'ethnic cleansing' of Native territories by a newly independent United States, from 1776 through to the end of the War of 1812.

Search for the route to the Great Salt Sea

The reward for good work, as they say, is more work. Four years later (1661), now with six children, Couture was approached by Governor Voyer d'Argenson to take part in an expedition being organized by Father Gabriel Druillettes, Claude Dablon, Denis Dablon and François Pelletier. The Governor's goal was to reassert French territorial and trade claims to the area that now comprises most of northern and western Québec and the Hudson Bay watershed of northern Ontario, an area of about half-a-million square miles, or the size of the States of Texas and California combined.

Couture may have seen this northwestern venture as being somewhat strategically misdirected. He certainly seemed to realize that the real future of 18th century North America was in the Great Lakes basin and beyond, into the Ohio valley and down the Mississippi. Over time, the

French authorities came to understand and embrace Couture's concept, too, especially after the Hudson's Bay Company demonstrated that it would not easily be dislodged. In the early 18th century, with the support of their growing network of western Native allies, the French pursued that vision with energy and remarkable, if unsustainable success.

Couture was a man of action, not politics nor philosophy. His insights were drawn from his open-minded perspective and his unique if rudimentary knowledge of the geo-politics of the Aboriginal world. In the west, the south and the northwest, the Iroquois and their western neighbours controlled an expanding array of territories. Having destroyed the Huron Wendat confederacy, the Iroquois were increasingly wealthy and well armed, initially by the Dutch and after 1664, by the English and their colonists. In addition to sallies against the French, the Iroquois relentlessly pressed the poor, scattered and relatively peaceable tribes of the north – ever further into limited, inhospitable lands and increasingly dangerous situations, in pursuit of the Iroquois goal of controlling the 'beaver trade' with the Europeans.

If the French could develop an alliance with the Iroquois, Couture knew that the French could move relatively easily and safely through the vast wilderness of eastern North America, as he did. Allied to the adversaries of the Iroquois hegemony, the French would be hemmed-in and overtaken by competition from Britain and the Netherlands, and their Aboriginal trade would be steadily diverted to British and Dutch merchants and settlers.

Despite these misgivings, Couture was ever a man of duty. Perhaps also lured by the siren of call of the adventures of his youth, Couture agreed to participate. The distinguished party of French explorers set-out from Québec, picking-up Native guides from the northern tribes on their way, and continuing up the Saguenay, across Lac-St-Jean and headed west. Benefitting from (and relying upon) their Native guides for provisions and logistical support, the French reached the height of land that divides the Atlantic watershed from that running west into James and Hudson Bays. They had journeyed hundreds of miles into territory unknown to Europeans, with the likely prospect of being able to better assert French territorial claims in their contest with the British traders.

At that point, however, almost to confirm Couture's premise, the Natives from the St. Lawrence valley recognized that this would mean moving into Cree territory and more importantly, put them in reach of the Iroquois war parties that were harassing all the northern tribes.

Despite frustrated efforts to make them change their minds, the wary Natives abandoned the few Frenchmen, leaving Couture and his compatriots no alternative but to retrace their watery path, east to the St. Lawrence. The threat anticipated by the northern tribes seems all the more remarkable when one considers the geography. A look at today's map demonstrates the amazing range achieved by the Iroquois war parties by this time, recognizing that they had no settlements north of the Great Lakes and traversed this vast, trackless wilderness by canoe.

A second expedition to the Northern Sea

In Paris, French authorities were becoming increasingly alarmed at the impact that the British and their new Native commercial allies were having on the French fur trade. A new Governor was dispatched, with instructions to reinvigorate the French commercial enterprise. Despite the lessons of the 1661 mission, the new Governor Dubois Davaugour was determined to repeat the foray, with more men and more provisions. And to ensure its success, he enlisted someone that everyone said was just the person to make the venture a success: Guillaume Couture.

One imagines the discussion that must have ensued at the little home on the Pointe-de-Lévy. Anne had just given birth to his namesake, Guillaume, on October 12, 1662.

But in early 1663, Governor Dubois issued a royal proclamation directing Couture to take command of the expedition and to accompany the..."*Indians northwards as far and as long as he shall deem it expedient for the service of the King and the good of the country: and he may go himself or send others to winter with them, if he thinks that his own safety may thereby be ensured and that some public advantage may ensue.*" [12]

Couture was not the sort of person to 'lead' a mission through others, and so in early summer 1663, he set out with Pierre Duquet and Jean Langlois at the head of an armada of 44 canoes, with Natives from a variety of tribes. The French authorities, including Couture, had reasoned that with

Couture in the lead and with sufficient numbers for protection, they had ensured a better prospect for success than in 1661. Despite their many Native companions, both French and Natives remained dependent on local tribes that they encountered on the way, to guide them through unknown rivers and portages, and often treacherous rapids along their route. More fundamentally, they misread the level of fear of the Iroquois among those northern tribesmen.

The party worked its way north through the Saguenay fjord and across Lac St.-Jean, then over the height of land that was the turn-around point in the failed mission of 1661. Conditions soon deteriorated, beginning with a heavy snowfall late in the month of June, impeding the progress of the flotilla of canoes and raising fears of 'bad omens' among all concerned. With Couture's urging, the party pressed on, forging across Lac Mistassini, and resting on a large offshore island where the blackflies were not as bad as on shore, and where the fishing remains great to this day. From that island, which now bears his name, the party sought-out the headwaters of the great Rupert River, and then on to Lac Nemiscau, from which the Rupert flows into James Bay's salt water.

At this point, however, local Cree guides were becoming reluctant to lead the group farther west, and many in the party were beginning to share their misgivings. Reports of local Iroquois activity were enough to halt progress and once again, to compel a retreat. The irony of the Iroquois projecting their influence into the vast wilderness of northern Québec and Ontario around James Bay must have confirmed Couture's long-held views. A comprehensive peace and collaboration with the Iroquois was the key to the success of New France, ironically even on its northern frontier.

Although not reaching salt water at the mouth of the Rupert, Couture could take satisfaction in having identified and reporting on a clear overland canoe-route to the Great Salt Sea. As two failed expeditions demonstrated, however, exploiting that route would need to be preceded either by peace with the Iroquois, or through the force of French arms. Ultimately, the course of arms prevailed – through raids on the English led by his friend Charles Le Moyne's legendary sons, along James and Hudson Bays. Although not evident at the time, the disappointing mission was not in vain. As part of later peacetime efforts to protect their claims to an expansive New France, the French Government's diplomatic case included a 1688 affidavit by Couture, attesting to the extent of his travels and discoveries in 1663, including the unchallenged claim to have explored the length of the Rupert River valley.

In 1668-69, funded and provisioned by key figures in the English Royal Court, the disgruntled New France explorers and fur-traders Pierre Radisson and Médard des Groseilliers explored the "tree line" coast from the Rupert River's mouth on James Bay, to the Nelson River in present-day Manitoba. Like Couture, des Groseilliers had lived with the Huron as a donné and like Couture, Radisson had been captured and then later 'adopted' by the Iroquois. Both moved through the wilderness with ease and familiarity. When Radisson and his elder brother-in-law des Groseilliers returned to England from the venture with a great and valuable quantity of furs, that was enough to encourage King Charles II to incorporate the Hudson's Bay Company in 1670, with the encouragement of James, the Duke of York and the Prince of Wales, Prince Rupert, both of whom left their names on the region's waterways.

With Prince Rupert as its first Governor, the Hudson's Bay Company quickly made good on the expansive charter awarded by King Charles, to the "Governor and Company of Adventurers of England Trading into Hudson's Bay". To the bemusement of the French, and typically without any consideration of the Native peoples whose land it was, the King had awarded the Hudson's Bay Company all the lands containing rivers flowing into Hudson Bay, a watershed of nearly four million hectares or one and a half million square miles. Few realized that this land grant covered an area a dozen times larger than Britain itself (then 125,000 square miles, including the Republic of Ireland). In fact, it represented 15% of North America, extending as far as present day Minnesota and Montana. But the French authorities certainly knew that it represented a bulwark against the northwestward expansion of their colony and siphoned-off the sources for their primary commercial enterprise, the increasing lucrative trade in furs to provide fashionable, waterproof headgear for the gentlemen of Europe and Britain.

New exploration assignments

Couture made clear his desire to be considered "retired from service" and to work his farm with his growing family. Colonial authorities, however, knew his great value and influence; they were reluctant to let

Couture withdraw from public life and wilderness exploration. For the next several years, Couture found himself routinely recruited each season for some mission of political or religious importance.

So it was that Couture was approached in 1665, when Father Henri Nouvel decided that he wished to lead an evangelization mission to the Papinachois nation, northeast of Couture's first New France home in Tadoussac. Nouvel had over-wintered in the Lac St-Jean area, but he wanted to push farther north. Now over 48 years of age, Couture agreed to undertake the expedition out of a sense of religious obligation, but only if he was be accompanied by some other experienced colonials. Charles Amiot, Noël Jérémie and Sébastien Prouvereau agreed to comprise the party.

Leaving in late May of 1665, but deprived of Native guides, they succeeded in reaching the proposed rendezvous point at the mouth of the Manicouagan River, near the vast meteor crater of Lake Manicouagan. But the Papinachois evidently had a change of heart and did not appear. So, Couture and his party turned back, returning to Québec on July 26, 1665, after enduring eight weeks of paddling and portaging across the mosquito- and black-fly-infested forests of central Québec.

A delicate mission to occupied New Netherlands

War with the Iroquois remained a constant threat for New France. Sustaining the peace while the Iroquois attacked New France's Native allies was also a diplomatic challenge for the French, especially when French missionaries often found themselves in the middle of raids by one Native band on another. Above all, there was the recurrent risk of an isolated incident escalating out of control, or being ignored and misread as weakness or lack of resolve on the part of the French. It was a delicate and volatile balance, especially with the highly distinctive and decentralized decision-making structure that 'governed' the Iroquois nations, particularly the Mohawks. Few understood this enigmatic equilibrium better than Couture.

In 1666, two French officers, including a Lieutenant Chazy, had been ambushed and murdered by a group of "freelancing" Mohawk braves, at a French outpost just inside Iroquois country and on the frontier claimed by

New Netherlands (a colony now occupied by the English). The incentive for a young man to demonstrate bravery and to challenge adversaries was (and remains) an important feature in Iroquois culture, even when Elders were cautioning restraint and cooperation. It was the kind of incident that could easily spin out of control, and plunge the French, the Iroquois, the English, and the Dutch settlers into unwanted mutual hostilities.

The French decided that they needed to make a demonstration of their resolve, but they were in no position to go to war – and they knew it. The Governor asked the forty-nine year-old Couture if he would intervene in this delicate diplomatic effort. After an emotional conversation with Anne, who would be left to care for their eight children, he agreed. In a highly risky gambit, Couture travelled directly into the heart of Iroquois territory, bearing a profoundly unwelcome message from the French. Once more, the fate of Couture was in the hands of the Iroquois and his fate was unknown to those waiting anxiously in New France.

Knowing the power and deference that the Mohawks showed to strong and compelling rhetoric, and trading on his reputation within the counsels of the Iroquois, Couture recalled his best and most forceful Mohawk dialect. He confronted the Mohawk leadership with the issue and persuaded them that in the absence of justice for the dead French soldiers, a punitive raid by the French army was the inevitable result. The Mohawk council conferred, without him.

On September 6, 1666, Couture re-appeared at Québec. Accompanying him were two Mohawk prisoners, with the astonishing consent of the Iroquois for the French to administer justice as they saw fit (knowing that likely meant a death penalty for murder). The colony's residents were immensely relieved. As a result of Couture's skill as a negotiator and as an orator, the colonial authorities had avoided a devastating war that might have spelled the end of the French in America. It was a triumph of Couture's influence with the Iroquois and it confirmed the prominence of this 'commoner' among the minor nobility and clergy who administered New France.

---

[12]   Dictionary of Canadian Biography, Vol. II, http://www.biographi.ca/en/bio/ couture_guillaume_1701_2E.html

---

CHAPTER 10

Different battles: roots and expansion

Sinking roots

With the triumphant return of Couture and his prisoners, and the peace commitment of the Iroquois, the colonial and religious authorities were finally prepared to accept Couture's desire to spend his time at home on Pointe-de-Lévy. Anne certainly shared that view. The 1667 census records that their little family had grown to include nine children, and unrecorded was that Ann was expecting their tenth. Their farm supported six head of cattle and fully twenty acres were now under cultivation. Couture was content with this retreat to a more placid lifestyle. There were mouths to feed and the farm needed his full-time attention.

The colonial authorities respected Couture's decision, but they did not forget about him. Couture was appointed the Clerk and later Judge of the local court and captain of the militia. By the mid-1680s, his self-taught literacy led him to work as a notary for his unlettered fellow residents of the growing south-shore Seigneury of Lauzon.

The French colonial authorities looked to a council of officers and minor nobility, the Sovereign Council, to advise a succession of Governors in exercising their royal mandate. It is noteworthy that the status-conscious colonial authorities routinely appointed Couture as a substitute member of the Sovereign Council, when permanent members were absent. In an early example of a practice that would become characteristic of America and Canada, the colonial authorities chose to overlook his humble origins and his lack of wealth and titled status, in order to benefit from his wisdom, experience and counsel on difficult problems.

Although we know little of his personality and his words are largely unrecorded, it is remarkable that Couture was not just the only non-Iroquois even accorded a seat on their governing council, but in a pre-revolutionary France where status mattered above all else, an uneducated commoner was routinely asked to sit on the Sovereign's Council for New France. His words, his experience and his force of character must have been indeed very compelling.

Father of the brides

Always devoutly religious, Couture petitioned in 1675 for a parish priest to serve their little community on the south coast, although a scarcity of priests deferred that parish assignment for some fifteen years. More practically, the church's archives record a succession of marriages of the Coutures' ten children: in 1678, Marie, age 20, married François Vézier, and upon his death, remarried to Claude Bourget in 1683; in 1680, Marguerite, age 22, married Jean Marsolet, son of the illustrious Nicolas Marsolet de Saint-Aignan; and, in 1688, seventy-one year-old Couture gave his daughter Louise, age 23, in marriage to the descendent of another original settler family Québec, Charles-Thomas Couillard de Beaumont.

One clerical footnote makes passing reference to the continuing piety of the former donné: In noting the lack of availability of venues suitable for a religious observances on the south shore, it is observed that *"...A sole chapel exists that can serve as a mother-church, the one built at St.-Joseph-de-la-Pointe-Lévy by Guillaume Couture in 1677, at the request of Abbot Morel"*.

A man who had achieved much through determination and self-assertion, Couture could be difficult neighbour, if he thought his rights encroached. The legal records of Sovereign Council suggest that his old partner and neighbour Byssot found Couture a litigious soul, perhaps even using his official capacities to assert personal interests.

Above all, however, Couture could also be relied upon in difficult times and never forgot his modest beginnings and his pride in his craft. In the 1681 census, he records himself not as a judge or a landowner, but as a simple carpenter with four guns and seven cattle.

The English raid of 1690

In the turbulent world of New France, conflict was never far away. If it was not the Iroquois, then it was the English. As the 17th century wore on, England's American colonists were added to the list of threats. Depending on the state of relations between England and France, the New Englanders' periodic royal commissions as 'privateers' provided legal sanction for raiding and piracy along the St. Lawrence and the Atlantic approaches to New France.

In 1690, Guillaume Couture was a seventy-three-year-old farmer with the honorific title of Captain of Militia. After many years of relative peace in the colony, the residents of the Lauzon coast saw little need for military defense or to drill militia, relying on French regulars at Québec to protect them and their families. As a result, palisades or fortifications no longer defended little colonial settlements near Québec, like Lévis.

But when the sails of the Phips privateers were cited rounding Orléans Island in the summer of 1690, south shore residents looked once more to Couture for leadership in time of peril.

As Wolfe's long siege of the town of Québec would later prove, its commanding geographic position required some ability to marshal forces and to attack from the safety of a protected base of deployment (and gunnery). Phips saw immediately that the river could offer defense to the French, but it could also offer protection to his men, who were crammed into wooden sailing ships in unfamiliar channels at a narrow point in the St. Lawrence. Couture's experienced eye read the mental map the same way from his wide, riverfront porch on Pointe-Lévy. If Phips could land his forces unmolested on the point, he could provision his men, train his guns on the town, and dash across the river in darkness when the time was ripe. If he could not, he would have to land in some less auspicious location, like Orléans Island, with the town out of range of his guns and risking his fleet in making an attack.

Few in the colony knew more about ambushes, from first-hand knowledge, than Guillaume Couture. Recognizing that a maritime assault force would benefit from a landing ground opposite their intended siege target – Québec – Couture guided younger, more able-bodied inhabitants – including his sons, such as 28-year old Guillaume – in making a show of presence and potential resistance that evidently dissuaded Phips from risking his ships or his crews with a contested landing on the Lauzon shore. Ultimately, the New Englanders realized that the enlistment promises of booty without much risk to life, limb or vessel would not be kept. They returned home after raiding a few outposts.

Retirement

With the departure of the Phips threat, Couture and Anne grew old together on their farm, celebrating the New Year with the first marriage of third son Guillaume to Madeleine Côté of nearby Beaumont, on February 7. His son Guillaume's marriage in 1691 to Madeleine was followed with the birth the following year of Couture's first grandchild, another "Guillaume", on June 8th, and 1696, on June 8th, by the birth of grandson Augustin, and then by three others, including Joseph. Fatefully, the birth of Joseph in February 1703 was followed quickly by the death of his mother. Couture's son Guillaume became a widower.

In the practical custom of the day, a forty-one year-old widower with four surviving children remarried soon afterwards, in July 1703, to Nicole Buffard, who bore him five more children, four of whom survived infancy. At fifty-one, Couture's son Guillaume again found himself a widower, and married Anne Adam, who delivered a remarkable nine children, eight of whose weddings during the 1740s and 1750s are recorded in church archives.

The Coutures were supported in their declining years by their youngest son, Joseph-Oger, born in 1670, who had affected the sobriquet, Sieur de la Cressonnière. In the last weeks of the century, Anne became ill. Although they saw in the new century together and marveled at the contribution they had made to establishing their family in the New World, Anne died soon after, on January 15, 1700. Appropriately, Guillaume and the ten children of her family buried their mother in a grave in the winter-hard ground of Pointe-de-Lévy, in view of Québec.

The loss of his wife took much of the spark out of the life of aging Guillaume. He got his affairs in order, transferring sum of 600 livres to his dutiful son Joseph-Oger on June 28th. Guillaume Couture died the following year, on April 4, 1701, at age 84, in the Hôtel-Dieu hospital in Québec City, perhaps from the smallpox epidemic of that year.

In keeping with traditional practice, on November 15th of the year of his death, a notary named Michel LePailleur prepared an inventory of Guillaume Couture's estate. The summary is a poignant testament to the man and his life. It betrays little indication of the immense impact that his life had on his times and on our history...

- Two small feather beds, with duck-down coverlets
- Several worn-out Norman-style shirts
- In the barn: three beef cattle, two yearling pigs, and a cow
- In the pantry: dishes, basins, plates, pots, old-tin spoons
- In the kitchen: a grill, a skillet, a caldron, two old kettles, and a fire-shovel
- In the house: a small copper compass, an eight-pound gun, a large axe, a long saw, and an auger
- On the property: an old plough, a sickle, a winnow, and several lengths of chain.

The Great Peace of Montréal

Very shortly after Couture's death, a remarkable development occurred. A party of Iroquois leaders who had heard from their fathers of "Achirra" and his tireless efforts to build friendship between the French and the Iroquois, made an overture to the French Colonial authorities. The Iroquois proposed that all those tribes and Nations, with whom Couture had advocated his case during their fathers' generation, and many others, should meet to discuss a comprehensive peace.

For the Iroquois, exhausted by generations of war, and more recently, by contagious disease and famine, it was a way to consolidate their gains and restore their villages. It would also allow them to shift their focus from subduing their Aboriginal neighbours to the immensely more challenging and complex tasks of coping with European settlement all around them, and playing-off the French against the English and their waves of American colonists.

In the spirit of Couture's vision, the Iroquois proposed a treaty – not just between the French and the Iroquois, or with the French and their Native allies or Christianized Natives – but with and among all the Nations in the wide spheres of influence of the French and Iroquois. If adopted, the treaty would ensure peaceful co-existence and free, unmolested passage for French traders, priests and explorers across a vast area of eastern and central North America. Above all, it would mean safety, security and trade for current and future settlers in New France. Strategically, in a period of chronic colonial hostilities, it would also keep the powerful, well-armed Iroquois Confederacy neutral in the recurrent global, imperial contests that pitted the French against the English. To add urgency, the English now held both New England and New Netherlands (renamed New York), and were pressing their claims to the extensive Hudson's Bay Company territories to the north and west of New France.

The Iroquois proposal was embraced enthusiastically by the French.

The French colonial authorities and Iroquois leaders sent out word, across the length and breadth of eastern North America, that they would enjoy safe-passage to meet at Ville-Marie on the island of Montréal, at the end of the summer. To the alarm of the English, the invitation resonated to a vast array of Native nations, beleaguered by decades of internecine warfare among themselves and with the Europeans. From as far as a thousand miles in all directions their leaders and wise men set-out for the grand assembly, convened by the man they called Onontio, the Governor of New France. After much debate and discussion, followed by peace-making and celebration, the Great Peace of Montréal was signed and 'marked' by a remarkable 1300 representatives of 39 eastern North America Native nations. It was signed on August 4, 1701, four months to the day after the death of Guillaume Couture.

The treaty cleared the way for a decade-and-a-half of relative peace and security, during which French colonial settlement in North America at last sank irreversible roots, across New France and to a more limited extent, across the vast area later called the Louisiana Purchase. More romantically, it gave birth to canoe-borne trade that flourished far into the interior of North America, down the Mississippi to New Orleans, west into the Missouri basin, and north into the Canadian North West.

In the end, the peace did not last. Within a half-century, despite periodic French and Native victories over the English and American settlers along the Mississippi, Ohio and Great Lakes frontiers, Québec fell to the English, in the small but historically momentous Battle of the Plains of Abraham. But French pioneer roots had enough time to go deeper and they survived. While he died on the eve of his great vindication in 1701, and his name is now long forgotten by most historians, Guillaume Couture's long-sought peace proved to be his most lasting bequest to a generation of Europeans and Aboriginals in eastern North America. The foundation he laid with persistence and advocacy changed the trajectory of history for 18th century America.

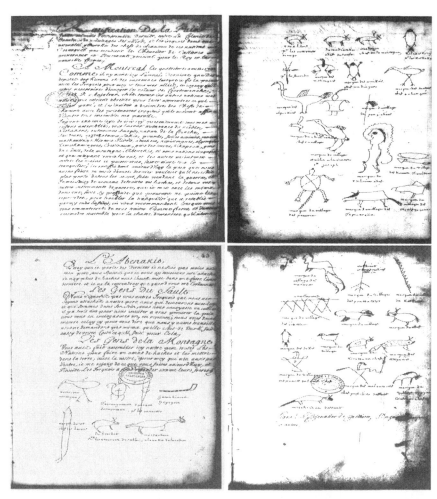

Chiefs' and delegates' signatures on the
Great Peace of Montréal – August 4, 1701
[Signatures des chefs autochtones
"Grande Paix de Montréal" – 1701]

© Archives nationales d'outre-mer, Aix-en-Provence
(ANOM, France) FR C11/19) Fonds des colonies,
c11a, vol. 19, fol 43-43v; COL C114 19/fol.41-44v

CHRONOLOGY OF EVENTS IN THE TIME OF GUILLAUME COUTURE

1600   Founding of permanent settlement at Tadoussac; only 5 of 16 French settlers survive first winter

1603   Champlain visits Tadoussac

1607   Jamestown Virginia established; First permanent British colony in North America

1608   Founding of Québec by Samuel de Champlain

1609   Champlain persuaded to support attack on Iroquois by Hurons and their allies, at Ticonderoga, in upstate New York. 'Modern' firepower allows Champlain to kill three Iroquois leaders, despite presence of only 5 French soldiers. 200 Iroquois warriors retreat, but century-long hostilities begin.

1609-1701 Iroquois launch the off-and-on "Beaver Wars" against the settlements of French and their Native allies – notably Huron (Wendat / Wyandotte) and other neighbouring Native Nations. Conquests by Iroquois include: Anishinabek (Algonquin, Ojibway); Hurons (defeated 1649); Mohicans (defeated/absorbed 1628); Neutrals (defeated/absorbed 1651); Petuns (defeated/absorbed 1650); Erie (defeated/absorbed 1657); Susquehannocks (defeated/absorbed 1680)

1617   Albany NY (Fort Orange) established by Dutch, at confluence of Mohawk and Hudson rivers. Trading post to serve Mohawk fur trade, and for transshipment to New Amsterdam harbour

1617   Guillaume Couture born in Rouen France

1620   Plymouth Massachusetts established by Pilgrims

1625   New Amsterdam (Fort Amsterdam), later New York City, founded by Dutch

1632   Champlain publishes *"Voyages from western New France, called Canada"* In 1633, population of Québec sinks to just 77 "permanent" French residents

1634   Iroquois and Huron reach a peace treaty, lasts to 1639; Jesuit Father Isaac Jacques establishes Ste-Marie-among-the-Hurons in present-day central Ontario

1635   Champlain dies on Christmas Day; Québec numbers only a few hundred permanent European residents

1637 (est.) Couture makes multi-week crossing of Atlantic and lands at Tadoussac

1639   **In October, Couture journeys with 18 French men to Ste-Marie-among-the-Hurons;** Huron Grand Chief "Eustache" Ahatsistari breaks 1634 peace treaty with Iroquois, with great victory over the Seneca Nation

1640   Beaver Wars begin in earnest, between the Iroquois and New France, including its Huron and Algonquin allies

1641   **Teenager Charles Le Moyne joins Couture at Ste-Marie-among-the-Hurons, for a four-year residency;** Le Moyne later father to Montréal family of 12 sons and 2 daughters, including Pierre d'Iberville, Jean-Baptiste de Bienville and Jacques Le Moyne

1641   **In June, Couture prepares and registers his Will, be-fore returning to Huronia; Couture again at Ste-Marie-among-the-Hurons for winter of 1641-42**

1642   **Couture journeys to Québec from Ste-Marie-among-the-Hurons in spring, setting-out for return in August 1642 with twenty-three others. Party ambushed and captured by Iroquois en route. Remaining members of French and Huron expedition marched to Upstate New York, followed by torture and execution. Couture survives; assigned to Iroquois war widow's family**

1643   **In November, Isaac Jacques escapes captivity with Couture's assistance, through Fort Orange and New Amsterdam; Couture remains captive of Iroquois;** Kleft's War (1643-45) between

Dutch settlers and local Native tribes around New York City area, ruinous war to secure Manhattan and environs for the Dutch

1645   **July 5, unrecognized Couture and Iroquois negotiators arrive at Trois-Rivières; July 12, Couture reveals himself and peace negotiations begin**

1646   **Couture's shuttle-diplomacy missions with Hurons and Iroquois;** late in year, two Jesuits murdered, peace initiative collapses

1647   **Couture "welcomed home" in Trois-Rivières celebration;** Peter Stuyvesant begins administration of New Netherland

1648   **Couture clears and settles Pointe-de-Lévy, opposite the town of Québec**

1650s   Rapid growth and expansion of New Netherland (1650s); First Anglo-Dutch War (1652-54)

1653   Peace invitation extended by the Onondagas (an Iroquois nation) to New France

1656   An expedition of Jesuits, led by Father Simon Le Moyne, establishes Sainte Marie de Ganentaa (near Syracuse NY)

1657   Peace treaty between New France and Iroquois (1657-58); **Couture commissioned by Governor to undertake peace initiative with Onondagas**

1658   The Jesuits forced to abandon Onondaga mission as hostilities with Iroquois resume

1658   Iroquois war party attacks Tadoussac, **occupying Couture's farm on the return voyage**

1660   Battle of the Long-Sault, west of Montréal, with New France militia and Aboriginal allies, against Iroquois; Dollard-des-Ormeaux, with Canadien militia, Hurons and Algonquins battle Iroquois, west of Montréal

1661   Pierre Le Moyne d'Iberville born to Charles LeMoyne; Future founder of Louisiana territory (Mississippi)

1661   **Couture leads expedition to Rupert River country in north-central Québec, looking for alternate route to James and Hudson Bays**

1663   **At Governor Dubois's direction, Couture repeats the expedition to find an alternate route to Hudson Bay, via the Rupert River**

1663　"Filles du Roi" arrive in New France, as potential brides for settlers; King creates Sovereign Council to govern New France; Québec elects a Mayor; Couture periodic member of Council

1664　New Netherland surrendered to British; New Amsterdam on Manhattan Island is largest European settlement in North America, comprising Dutch, Africans, British and others

1665　Carignan-Salières Regiment arrives from France to provide security for New France; Québec has 550 residents in 70 houses, 25% clergy

1665　Couture accepts commission to lead overland expedition into remote northeastern Québec (Papinachois Nation), beyond Tadoussac

1666　Census records 3,215 settlers in New France. During the autumn, the soldiers of Carignan-Salières, led by Alexandre de Prouville, the "Marquis de Tracy" and the Governor, including Charles Le Moyne, invade the Iroquois territory to the south, burn five of their main towns and destroy their crops.

1666　Two French officers murdered by Iroquois on border between New France and British-occupied New Netherland; **Couture leads a mission to the hostile Iroquois, to retrieve the killers; Couture returns triumphal in September, with the killers as prisoners**

1667　Census records that Guillaume Couture and Anne Esmart now have nine children on their farm at Point-de-Lévy

1668　Radisson explores James Bay for the British

.1670　Hudson's Bay Company established; **Son Joseph-Oger born to Coutures**

1673　New Netherland re-taken by Dutch from British

1674　New Netherland finally lost to British; renamed New York

1675　King Philip's War begins (across New England)

1677　Couture erects a chapel at Lévis

1678　Coutures' daughter Marie, 20, marries

1680　Coutures' daughter Marguerite, 22, marries

1682　Rene Cavalier de la Salle claims the Mississippi Valley for King Louis of France

1683　Coutures' widowed daughter Marie re-marries

1684　Pierre Esprit Radisson goes to work for the Hudson's Bay Company and the British

1685 Charles Le Moyne dies at Montréal, age 59 (in his youth, he was a fellow resident with Couture at Ste-Marie-among-the-Hurons)

1686 Charles's son, Jacques Le Moyne leads successful attacks on Hudson's Bay Company forts

1687 Jacques Le Moyne leads Aboriginal contingent in attack on Iroquois Seneca Nation; French military (Denonville) raids on Seneca homeland of Iroquois destroy 1.2 million bushels of corn

1688 King William's War begins (1688-1697)

1688 Coutures' daughter Louise, 23, marries

1689 The first French and Indian war, King William's War begins. Jacques Le Moyne attacks Hudson's Bay forts and seizes British ships; Lachine Massacre takes place

1690 Phips' raid on Québec; elderly Couture captain of militia defending south shore; ~~Québec has 550 residents in 70 houses, 25% clergy~~

1690 King William's War continues

1691 King William's War continues; ~~During the autumn, the soldiers of Carignan-Salières, led by Alexandre de Prouville, the "Marquis de Tracy" and the governor, including Charles Le Moyne, invade the Iroquois territory to the south, burn five of their main towns and destroy their crops.~~

1691 Coutures' son Guillaume marries Madeleine Côté; ~~Couture leads a mission to the hostile Iroquois, to retrieve the killers of French soldiers; Couture returns triumphal in September, with the killers as prisoners~~

1692 June 8, Madeleine and Guillaume (Jr.) have son, also named Guillaume; grandson to Guillaume and Anne

1696 King William's War continues

1697 King William's War ends; **Son Joseph-Oger born to Coutures**

1698 June 8, Madeleine Côté & Guillaume Couture (Jr.) have son, Coutures' grandson Augustin

1699 Charles LeMoyne's son, Pierre Le Moyne d'Iberville establishes France's first permanent settlement in 'Louisiana', southern Alabama

1701 January 18, Couture's wife, Anne Esmard dies at Pointe-de-Lévy

1701 **April 4: Guillaume Couture dies at the Hotel-Dieu Hospital in Québec, age 84; November 15, Couture's Will probated**

1701   Great Peace of Montréal; August 4: Signing of the Great Peace of Montréal between 39 First Nation tribes, represented by 1300 Native delegates and the French Colonial government.

1701   Jean-Baptiste Le Moyne de Bienville, first appointed Governor of Louisiana; Cadillac founds Detroit; Jean-Baptiste Le Moyne de Bienville, son of Charles LeMoyne, re-appointed Governor of Louisiana on four occasions, through 1743, including replacing Cadillac in 1716, and establishing New Orleans (1718)

1702   Queen Anne's War (Spanish Succession) (1702-1713)

1704   Queen Anne's War continues; February 29 - Deerfield Massacre: French forces from Québec and Native American forces under the command of Jean-Baptiste Hertel de Rouville attacked village of Deerfield, Massachusetts.

1705   Despite ongoing hostilities between France and Britain, including their surrogates in New England, New York, New France and Louisiana, New France enjoys relative peace with all north-eastern, mid-western and Mississippi valley Native Nations. As a result, New France traders spread commercial and social networks and alliances across eastern and central North America.

1712   Queen Anne's War (Spanish Succession) continues; due to combination of non-belligerence treaties with Native Nations and success in battle against British and colonial forces, New France now extends from Newfoundland to Lake Superior and from the Hudson Bay to the Gulf of Mexico.

1713   Treaty of Utrecht; after eleven years of fighting, the signing of the Treaty of Utrecht ends Queen Anne's War between France and Great Britain. Acadia transferred to Britain with protection of Acadian rights; Cape Breton (Louisbourg) stays French. By the end of Queen Anne's War, French colonists in all of North America have grown to more than twelve thousand, although British colonists number almost one million

1743   Louis-Joseph Gaultier de La Vérendrye and his brother, François de La Vérendrye, travelling from Fort La Reine (now

Portage-La-Prairie, Manitoba), reach the Rocky Mountains, via the Yellowstone and Upper Missouri rivers

1744-1748 King George's War (Austrian Succession); 1745: Fortress of Louisbourg (Cape Breton Is.) seized by British; in 1748, Treaty of Aix-la-Chapelle restores Cape Breton, but not Acadia, to France

1754 Census records New France's population has grown to 55,009, while Atlantic seaboard 13 British Colonies now have a population over 1,170,800

1755 British begin Expulsion of Acadians, to elsewhere in North America, including Acadians settled in French Louisiana

1756-1763 French and Indian War (Seven Years War); Marquis Louis-Joseph de Montcalm takes command of forces at Québec 1757; The French army takes British Fort William Henry on Lake Champlain (now Upstate New York) on August 9.

1758: Montcalm's troops, with the assistance of the Duke of Lévis, and despite being outnumbered four-to-one, maul British at Ft. Carillon (Ticonderoga)

1759 Cherokee War begins (1759-61)

1759 British capture Québec; Montcalm and Wolfe both killed on the Plains of Abraham 1763 Treaty of Paris: France abandons New France, which becomes part of British North America; King George III's Royal Proclamation of 1763 guarantees rights of all Native Nations of Great Lakes Basin and west of the Appalachians.

EPILOGUE

What's in a name?

Guillaume and Anne had ten children, and in the Québec custom lasting into the mid-20th century, many of the subsequent generations of "Coutures" had large families, too. Descendents with the name "Couture" (or in some cases, Anglicized versions of it) now number in the thousands across North America. Surprisingly, given the number of children born to Anne and Guillaume, those who bear the Couture name are all descendants from their fourth son, also named Guillaume.

There are likely tens of thousands more "Couture" descendants, descended from the four original Couture daughters and – intriguingly – from the four of the five Couture boys recorded as married, but who in the custom of the era, adopted other surnames during the lifetime of their father and mother (Lamonde, La Cressonnière, Lafresnaie, and Bellerive).

There may be others. We recall that the twenty-eight year-old, unmarried Couture conspicuously requested release from his vow of celibacy before returning to his adopted Iroquois family and to Huronia, beginning in 1645.

Tracing family roots

Although political correctness sometimes frowns on its use, Quebeckers have a phrase: "Pûre laine de souche", to describe those who can trace their family to the original settlers. ("Pûre laine", meaning literally pure wool, or in English usage, "dyed in the wool", and "de souche" meaning from "old stock" or the original source). But how successful can one be in tracing family roots, when fires take church records and economic conditions spread families across the breadth of North America, often changing their family language as they do?

Can a family trace its roots back that far, despite the fires, floods and neglect of archives that spans three hundred and seventy-five years of American and Canadian history? Remarkably, the Coutures can do that.

BIBLIOGRAPHY

Couture, Pierre, *Guillaume Couture: Le Routurier Batisseur*, XYZ Editeur (Montréal QC: 2005)

Dictionary of Canadian Biography Online (Vol. II):

http://www.biographi.ca/009004-119.01-e.php?id_nbr=724

University of Toronto / Université de Laval (Toronto: 1966 [original print edition])

Huronia Historic Parks, *Images of Ste-Marie*, Huronia Historic Parks (Midland ON: 1989)

Roy, Joseph-Edmond, *Guillaume Couture, Premier Colon de la Pointe-Lévy (Lauzon)*, Mercier & Cie. (Lévis QC: 1884); reprinted for 1947 anniversary with introduction by Father Richard Couture, vicar of Notre-Dame de Québec

Reuben Gold Thwaites (ed.), *The Jesuit Relations and Allied Documents: Travels and Explorations of the Jesuit Missionaries in New France 1610-1791*, Burrows Brothers Company, Publishers (Cleveland OH: 1898); [Public Domain]

Trigger, Bruce G., *Natives and Newcomers – Canada's 'Heroic Age' Reconsidered*, McGill-Queen's University Press (Kingston ON and Montréal QC: 1986)

Sources:

Political and Social Division, Library and Archives Canada

550, boul. de la Cité, 7-76, Gatineau, QC Canada K1A 0N4

http://www.collectionscanada.gc.ca

(The 'fonds des colonies', series C11A, which contains the correspondence between the Governor and Intendant of New France and the Minister of Marine in France; Couture's trip to the Hudson's Bay area was often mentioned in the letters and reports (supporting French claims). The originals of those documents are held in the French Government's National Overseas Archives (Archives nationales d'outre-mer) in Aix-en-Provence, France.)

Bibliothèque et Archives nationales du Québec, Québec, QC

http://www.banq.qc.ca/accueil/ http://pistard.banq.qc.ca/unite_chercheurs/recherche_simple

(Many notarial records, including Guillaume Couture's marriage contract)

ENDNOTE
ON TERMINOLOGY

There are a number of ways in which we have come to describe the original inhabitants of North America, after Columbus first misnamed them "Indians". Usage in the United States differs from that of Canada, and the descendents of those original inhabitants also have preferences in naming themselves and their various sub-groups that may or may not have universal acceptance, even among themselves. The term "Indian" remains in widespread use, especially in the United States, and is a feature of much legislation and the names of organizations with a long history, like the Federation of Saskatchewan Indian Nations or the Eastern Band of Cherokee Indians. However, other terminology is commonly preferred.

The term "Aboriginal" embraces all original inhabitants of North America, including the Inuit (formerly known as Eskimo) and Labrador Innu, as well as those whose ancestry includes intermarriage with early residents of European and African origin, such as the Métis in Canada or the Seminole in Florida. Increasingly, there is a preference for the term "Indigenous" to describe the original inhabitants of North America, as well as their counterparts in Australia, New Zealand, Arctic Scandinavia, Greenland and northern and eastern Russia, and similar peoples.

In Canada, the more common terminology is "First Nations", although that term specifically excludes Inuit, Innu, and Métis, and also does not include those not officially associated or registered with a recognized First Nation (such as so-called "urban Aboriginals" or "non-status Indians"). In the United States, the original inhabitants are generally referred to as "Native Americans" or simply "Native", both by themselves and in popular usage.

For purposes of this narrative, the term "Native" will be used, since it is the most commonly used term across North America and it is the most easily understood and defined. Occasionally, the term "Aboriginal" will be employed, but its broad embrace of all original inhabitants should be understood from the context.

Recognized groups of Natives in the United States, at the level of linguistic or cultural groups are generally referred to as Nations, such as the Cherokee Nation or the Navajo Nation. In the past, such groups might have been described as Tribes, and notably in the United States, that use continues in some areas and in some contexts, such as legislation and literature. "Nations" often extend over a wide or even unrelated geographical area, whereas local or regional communities of Native Nations are recognized as Bands. Commonly, a Band is associated with one or more legally recognized Reserves, arising out of Treaties with American or British / Canadian governmental authorities in the 18th, 19th and 20th centuries.

In Canada, "Nations" may be a political or cultural affiliation, or a Treaty-based geographical grouping, but not a recognized First Nation. An example would be the Nishnawbe-Aski Nation (NAN) covering much of Northern Ontario, or a sub-set of NAN, the Mushkegowuk Tribal Council of Cree in Northeastern Ontario, both of which are made up of a voluntary association of often very small but legally recognized First Nation communities. First Nations generally have the legal authority to act for the registered members of the Band, whether those individuals are resident on recognized Reserves, or in predominantly Native communities within their traditional territory, or resident elsewhere in the country, including in a major urban centre.

In all instances, the history of a Native Nation influences the understanding of the terms used to describe them. The Six Nations of the Iroquois and the Civilized Tribes of Oklahoma include Native groups that consider themselves distinct from one another, but which are united for some purposes, in much the way that Italians or Germans would consider themselves Europeans for some political, economic, legal or social purposes.

For purposes of this book, the term "Nation" has been used to describe recognized groupings of Native people who share a common political and cultural heritage, such as the Huron / Wendat. The term "Nation" will also be used to describe distinct sub-groups with a recognized independent history and identity, such as the Seneca Nation or the Mohawk Nation, in which case terms like "Confederacy" has been employed to describe their affiliation with the Iroquois. While the terms "tribe" or "band" may be used in context, the more commonly employed term of "community" will be used to describe local settlements of individual Nations.

It should also be noted that, while each Nation is subdivided geographically into communities, the more culturally sophisticated Nations might also have a robust tradition of Clans, which transcend Nations within broader cultural groups, like the Iroquois or the Huron. Members of the Bear Clan or the Turtle Clan may maintain an affiliation that cuts across other cultural boundaries. Historically, clan-affiliation proved to be important in a matriarchal society, in such areas as selection of spouses or Elders' decisions about leadership succession. Extended family affiliation often remains a major factor in elections for Band Council representatives within smaller Native communities, as is common in other global societies where "clan" affiliation is an important ingredient in democratic choice.

CPSIA information can be obtained at www.ICGtesting.com
Printed in the USA
LVOW06s0050190915

454879LV00001B/177/P

9 781483 432649